RESOURCE BOOKS FOR TEACHERS

series editor
ALAN MALEY

D0530667

CLASS READERS

Jean Greenwood

Oxford University Press

Oxford University Press
Walton Street, Oxford OX2 6DP

Oxford   New York   Toronto
Delhi   Bombay   Calcutta   Madras   Karachi
Petaling Jaya   Singapore   Hong Kong   Tokyo
Nairobi   Dar es Salaam   Cape Town
Melbourne   Auckland

and associated companies in
Berlin   Ibadan

Oxford, Oxford English and the *Oxford English logo* are trade marks of
Oxford University Press

ISBN 0 19 437103 4

Set by Pentacor Limited, High Wycombe, Bucks

Printed in Hong Kong.

Acknowledgements

I am indebted to Dorothy Heathcote, formerly of Newcastle University, who first introduced me to the concept of framed teaching. Without her guidance and clarity a great many of these activities would have remained untaught.

I also wish to acknowledge all the teachers and students who have helped me in the development and trials of many of the activities: County High School, Chelmsford; Eurocentre, Bournemouth; Pagoulatou-Vlachou School, Athens. Especial thanks go to the Rovolas School, Athens, and also to my colleagues at the British Council, Athens, for their moral support and to my students for their encouraging responses.

Finally, my thanks go to Christopher Kennedy whose tolerance, generosity and good humour enabled me to concentrate on writing.

Acknowledgements are also made to the following for their permission to include published material:

Heinemann Educational Books for book cover from *Animal Farm* by George Orwell, illustrations from *Rich Man – Poor Man* by T C Jupp and quotations from *The Stranger* by Norman Whitney; Longman for book cover from *Animal Farm* and illustrations and quotations from 'Lord Mountdrago' by W Somerset Maugham, 'The Courtship of Susan Bell' by Anthony Trollop, 'The Doll's House' by Katherine Mansfield and 'The Man Who Could Work Miracles' by H G Wells (all from *Outstanding Short Stories*); Oxford University Press for quotations from *Space Affair* by Peter Viney and pictures from *Tales from the Arabian Nights* retold by Rosemary Border and *The Piper of Hamelin* retold by Anthony Toyne; Penguin Books for book cover from *Animal Farm*; and the estate of the late Sonia Brownell Orwell and Secker & Warburg Ltd. for extracts from *Animal Farm*.

Illustrations by Alex Brychta

Lettering artist: Elitta Fell

The publishers would like to thank the following for permission to reproduce photographs:
Mike Abrahams – *Network*; John Sturrock – *Network*
Location photographs by Rob Judges and Mark Mason.

Contents

Section C: After reading

The author and series editor

Jean Greenwood graduated in 1973 and taught English in secondary schools in Essex, England for seven years. From 1982 she worked in Greece and from 1985–1987 she was a Senior teacher and teacher-trainer with the British Council, Athens. In 1984 her book *Light Reading* was written and published in Greece to accompany the reintroduction of First Certificate Prescribed Texts. From 1985–1987 she served on the Board of TESOL Greece as vice-chairman and editor of their magazine. She has lectured in Germany and Mexico and is also known in Greece as a speaker and lecturer for the Pan-Hellenic Association of Language School Owners. She is currently a freelance teacher-trainer and writer.

Alan Maley worked for The British Council from 1962–1988, serving as English Language Officer in Yugoslavia, Ghana, Italy, France, and China, and as Regional Representative for the British Council in South India (Madras). He is currently Director-General of the Bell Educational Trust, Cambridge.

He wrote *Quartet* (with Françoise Grellet and Wim Welsing, Oxford University Press (OUP) 1982). He has also written *Beyond Words, Sounds Interesting, Sounds Intriguing, Words, Variations on a Theme,* and *Drama Techniques in Language Learning* (all with Alan Duff), *The Mind's Eye* (with Françoise Grellet and Alan Duff), and *Learning to Listen* and *Poem into Poem* (with Sandra Moulding). He is also Series Editor for the Oxford Supplementary Skills Series.

Foreword

Shortened, simplified, abridged and adapted – Readers have been with us from the dim mists of primeval English Language Teaching (ELT), where the wraith of Michael West can still be seen flitting through the swamps. They continue to be published in considerable numbers. Presumably therefore, teachers continue to buy them. But how they are used is not quite clear: as homework tasks; as open-access material in class libraries and resource centres; as material for the damp and dreary Friday afternoon session; or simply to prop open the door or decorate a shelf?

Here is a book which addresses this problem squarely. Highly original in its conception, it treats the Reader as a total language learning resource, not simply as a device for promoting reading. This book is about exploiting Readers in every possible way, not simply about using them to 'teach' reading. The Reader is conceived of as a springboard to propel the learner into manifold language learning activities, rather than a couch upon which he or she can passively recline.

The author offers a cornucopia of varied activities for teachers to try. All are based upon her own extensive classroom experience. Some may seem unfamiliar, or even alien, to some teachers. Tastes develop with exposure however, and after trying some of the more familiar tasks, even the more reticent teachers may be encouraged to experiment with some of the less conventional activities. This is, after all, not a pre-set menu, but a cookery book where you can choose the recipe which suits your palate best. Its chief characteristic is that it promotes exploration and experiment, even at the most basic level.

To the perceptive reader it will have important, and arguably revolutionary, implications for the teaching of literature. Readers are often the first point of exposure of the English as a Foreign Language (EFL)/English as a Second Language (ESL) student to literature. The activities on offer here encourage the development of *response* to text, not simply analysis. They also lead students to a personalized access to the 'literariness' of texts through a wider range of activities than is customary.

This is an exciting and challenging book. We hope and believe that teachers will respond to its challenge.

Alan Maley

Introduction

Throughout this book Reader refers to book, and reader refers to student.

Attitudes to Readers

The Reader has long been the black sheep of the EFL classroom. Teachers either ignore Readers, or neglect and abuse them, failing to recognize their learning potential. The reason for this can no longer be laid at the door of the publishers. Nowadays, a vast range of material is produced suitable for all interests, age ranges, and ability levels. It is more probably the attitude of the teacher, and thus, the student which is responsible. Are any of the following close to your own attitude, or familiar to you from conversations with colleagues?

'Readers are an expensive luxury. The school cannot afford them. Other things must come first.'

'I am trying to get through a fairly dense syllabus to equip my students, ultimately, for examinations, I cannot spare the time for frills.'

'Reading for pleasure is a private and personal thing. I cannot see how this can be used in the EFL classroom.'

'I understand that extensive reading for pleasure can only improve language, but I have no way of checking that learning has taken place other than comprehension questions. These activities reduce the pleasure.'

The above are explanations, excuses, reasons and justifications from teachers talking about the scant use of Readers in the classroom. Their comments illustrate three views prevalent at present. First, that teachers feel that time spared for Readers will in some way deprive their students of certain key language skills and abilities. Second, that teachers are fostering or even pandering to students' reluctance to read for pleasure. Finally, that teachers are unaware of how to use and exploit Readers in their classrooms and, therefore, provide a limited range of activities which, in turn, limits the responses of their students. If teachers take Readers into the classroom with any one, or a combination of the above attitudes, this will be imparted to the students who will then also believe that Readers are preventing them from doing something more important, and are a waste of valuable learning time, or a chore, read only to enable them to answer a comprehension task.

The aims of this book

This book is an attempt to change the attitudes of both teachers and students to classroom activities involving Readers. The teacher who is worried that students will be missing something important will find included in the book activities which develop intensive and extensive reading skills, listening activities, writing in a variety of styles and registers, and oral tasks involving varying degrees of subtlety. Students are also encouraged to interpret, criticize, and extend what has been written, transfer information, and perform guided writing tasks. Functions of suggestion, persuasion, argument, and disagreement are practised, among others. Vocabulary tasks, letter, report and summary writing, problem-solving and picture-inspired discussion, all of which are examination required skills, are all shown to be possible with a Reader as the stimulus. The teacher who brings Readers into the classroom is not depriving the students of language practice, but is, instead, providing a richer context for such practice.

Unwilling readers

Reluctant readers are a problem in all types of classroom at present. This reluctance stems from a variety of social causes, or pressures on the student. In some countries, especially eastern Mediterranean countries, secondary age students are burdened with extremely heavy reading lists for homework. Reading is, therefore, associated with memorizing and regurgitating, and hard work. Taking a set of Readers into such a class of students and presenting them with still more words to be read will understandably produce displays of reluctance. The teacher may be tempted to adopt the system that the students are familiar with elsewhere and insist that the reading is done to enable them to answer questions at the next lesson. Such a system is self-destructive. Reading is no longer a pleasurable activity, and the teacher, aware that learning is taking place on a cognitive level only, may reluctantly be forced to abandon the attempt altogether, knowing that it is accomplishing very little of the intended original aim.

Less academic students are also unwilling, or reluctant readers. Reading is, for them, a passive, boring activity, performed constantly in isolation and perhaps associated with skills which they feel they do not possess. The 1970s and '80s are rapidly spawning a generation who, given free time, prefer to fill it with either the quick thrill of video, or the cheap thrill of comics and cartoon strips. The result will be a population incapable of reflection or contemplation – skills theoretically available to all academic levels – who prefer to be bombarded with the powerful visual images produced by others and who are incapable of producing their own images in either L1 or L2; a vulnerable generation.

As teachers we can either pander to the reluctant reader, or attempt to modify and enhance the view the student has of both reading for pleasure and, thereby, Readers.

Motivation and pleasure

It is up to the teacher to convince the reluctant reader that reading, either extensive or intensive, is pleasurable. Only one of many ways of obtaining pleasure is to be able to answer the teacher's comprehension check questions the following day. Such pleasure is fleeting as ultimately the teacher and the motivation of the comprehension questions will be removed. The world of reading will remain, and still be as inaccessible as ever to the student. The Reader and eventually, it is hoped, the unsimplified authentic text provide a means for the student to keep in touch with the foreign language long after the completion of the course. After we have learnt to drive and finally acquired our driving licences it would be perverse to then stop driving immediately and never to set foot in an automobile again, claiming that the licence alone was our goal. Yet, this is the attitude that we foster among our students. We enable them to obtain a 'licence' or certificate after examinations or tests and then, in the majority of cases, we deprive them of the interest, or ability to continue contact with the second language. (This excludes the minority of students who will be using L2 daily in some professional context.)

More rewarding than the fleeting pleasure of the correct answer and the narrow language skill that this demonstrates and practises, is to grant the students access to the world of the Reader and enable them to perceive the writer's skill or aims, while practising a wider range of language tasks. The writer's skill is demonstrated in Graded Readers and Simplified Texts as well as in authentic texts. Part of the pleasure of reading is to use the ability to appreciate, for example, theme, plot, setting, and characterization, and to have the confidence to trust one's own perceptions about what has been written and to voice one's ideas if required. These skills are most fully developed and refined with authentic texts, but the world of the authentic text and its language may not be immediately accessible to the foreign student. The initial steps towards this world can be taken through Readers. I am not necessarily advocating literary analysis in language classes; this would terrify more students than it would encourage. The activities in this book are all language based, but they also give students the chance to explore, at their own level, the way an author has developed character, etc. and provide opportunities to voice their views without fear of failure. When teachers use Readers they are often too concerned with *what* was written at the expense of *how*. Reading in any language is an affective as well as a cognitive process.

One way to encourage reluctant readers is to show them that reading can also be fun and give rise to a variety of interaction. The pre-reading stage should rarely, if ever, be omitted, for it is then that the students' curiosity to read is aroused. This can be done through a game based on their response to key vocabulary as in activity A7.1, or a project such as activity A3.2, or by transposing the world of the Reader into a form which is more recognizable, such as the magazine problem page in activity A4.2, or by giving students a problem to solve as with the news headlines in activity A2.5, or with a role play as in activity A4.1 where students respond to first impressions of characters and provide faces suitable to play the roles found in the Reader, while they themselves role-play as a studio casting department.

The activities in this book encourage students to respond to language subjectively, as well as objectively, and also allow them to interact. The communication takes place, not to arrive at a right answer, but to give a hearing to a variety of different ones. The teacher's role is not that of corrector or judge, but rather that of enabler. Teachers must, therefore, avoid the temptation to voice their own perceptions at the expense of those of the students, as they will automatically be judged, rightly or wrongly, to be the correct ones, and group interaction will be nullified. The teacher assists with language errors, but should not replace the students' perceptions with his or her own. In almost all the activities an opportunity exists for the teacher to check and assist the students' language learning without repressing the students' perceptions of what they are reading.

Accessibility

The presence of 'open' activities will also encourage the reluctant reader. 'Closed' activities are those which have a definite answer in mind at their onset, whereas 'open' activities simply have a series of different ones. If the students can recognize and communicate their perceptions about the Reader the activity is valid in an EFL classroom, whether or not these perceptions are shared by the teacher or by the majority of the class. If reading becomes associated with the opportunity to air views without penalty, then motivation to read is also fostered. A great many of the activities have been designed to enable the students to make conclusions of their own rather than to reach a particular pre-ordained conclusion.

Closely linked with the ideas above is the view some students have of reading for pleasure as intellectually artistic and, therefore, involving linguistic skills beyond their grasp. If students recognize the Reader to be a simplified version of a literary work they may well lack confidence in their own ability to criticize, comment, or interpret in a foreign language. This should not prevent the teacher from taking such Readers into the classroom. However, in order to make the world of the Reader accessible, the teacher may well have to renounce all his or her vows of 'purity' regarding creative literary writing. It is infinitely preferable to tear or cut a book up into pieces and present it in a more palatable, or dynamic form, if it will make this and subsequently other texts more accessible to the students, than to insist on a traditional reading which leaves the student 'cold'. Respect for the author is all very well, but not at the expense of the reader. Using Readers should always be viewed as a long term teaching investment and not as a short term input.

Extensive and intensive reading

The skills required to read with depth and, therefore, with pleasure have to be nurtured. They do not develop overnight, nor can they develop if students are instantly expected to read extensively simply because a class library has been organized. Teachers frequently complain that class libraries are time-consuming to organize and rarely worth the effort. Students take their first book home with a flush of enthusiasm, their second with grudging curiosity, and their third with an air of resignation; and this third book seldom, if ever, is read or returned, unless the teacher has kept a vigilant administrative eye over the library.

The failure of so many class libraries can be attributed to the over expectation of the teachers that students can develop reading and interpretative skills and a pleasure from reading within a vacuum, without encouragement or guidance. Class libraries or extensive reading programmes should also be accompanied by the intensive reading activities necessary if students are to develop any interpretative ability or awareness of the possibilities available in their second language. In other words, activities to develop, foster, and practise these skills should take place in the classroom, and be supplemented by a carefully chosen, readily available class library for after lesson hours.

The range of activities available to the teacher who embarks on intensive reading is large: from role play to card games, from matching tasks to Snakes and Ladders board games, from creating documents to playing Bingo. The age range of the students and their ability, and the enthusiasm of the teacher for the activity will dictate their success. What the activities mostly have in common is the students' close involvement with each other and with the Reader, and the acknowledgement of the use of Readers as part of a process, rather than as a product to be measured by the yardstick of comprehension questions or number of Readers superficially consumed within a school year.

How to use this book

This book is essentially a resource book of ideas. To exemplify these ideas reference has been made to specific Readers in the hope that teachers will adapt the activities for use with the Readers of their own, or their students' choice. In order to assist teachers, summaries of the Readers used for exemplification can be found in the Appendix at the end of the book.

The book consists of three major sections: A Pre-reading; B While Reading; C After Reading. Teachers are advised to use all three stages when planning a syllabus. The pre-reading stage whets the students' appetites and stimulates curiosity. The while reading stage increases the students' awareness and encourages them to look more closely at the Reader before its completion, and also enables the teacher to gauge how successful the Reader is and perhaps modify and adapt aims and pace. The after reading stage encourages reflection upon what has been read and enables the students to expand and enhance their perceptions. All three stages provide opportunity for communication and interaction between the students.

Within each major section there are various subsections, all of which contain a family of related activities dealing with one aspect of a Reader, for example, plot, characterization, theme, setting, etc.

The activities within each subsection are not graded, for example, activity A4.2 is not necessarily more difficult than activity A4.1. The order within each major section is not exactly arbitrary, but does not prescribe any order for a teacher to follow. Nor should a teacher feel that an activity from every subsection is necessary when drawing up a syllabus. The subsections refer simply to the variety of the activity available and do not indicate any sort of progression.

Section D deals with 'frame' and how altering the students' frame or perspective can alter the way the students respond both emotionally and linguistically to what they have read. A further explanation of this concept is found in the section itself.

Section E provides a sample programme for a short story. This is simply one of many possible programmes for the same story. It is intended as a guideline and should not be rigidly applied to all short stories, nor to all Readers.

The suggested times for the activities are also only guidelines. Teachers may find that they need more or less time according to the difficulty of the Reader, the level of the class, and the interest they display. The interest level of the students is a key factor in determining how long to spend on an activity or on a Reader.

The variety and unfamiliarity of some of the activities may be disturbing to some teachers. Every single activity has been attempted successfully in a classroom setting, which may reassure some teachers. The variety is necessary because of the variety of teachers, students, Readers, and classroom realities. Some of the activities included may work best with adult classes, some activities would be best for short intensive courses with multilingual classes, others work best on long courses where a continued relationship with the teacher or the school will increase success. Others would be most useful for the ESL teacher who, within the framework of a state school system, has a class of foreign students and a back-up of inter-departmental support.

To teachers of other languages

All the activities could be adapted for use by teachers of languages other than English, who have a range of Readers published in the target language.

To teachers of English as a first language

These activities could also be adapted for use by teachers of English to native speaker students of English within the English primary and secondary systems.

Conclusion

The apparent strangeness of some of the activities is perhaps due to our memories of the ossifying way Readers were used in our own L1 or L2 learning experiences. It is only recently that the 'Inner Worlds' of the reader/Reader have been acknowledged and exploration of, and creative response to text encouraged. Both teachers and students need to be stimulated when dealing with text, and the initial strangeness or novelty of some activities is an advantage to both in an area where predictablity of activity has led to predictability of response; stultifying for teachers and students alike. Teachers and students find shallow, anaemic reading dissatisfying and the motivation provided by unusual and unexpected tasks is necessary if our students' reluctance to read is not to be matched and augmented by our own unenthusiastic approach to the concept of developing the skills necessary to maximize the pleasure of reading.

Section A
Pre-reading

Pre-reading

Introduction

Interest in a Reader cannot be assumed and the teacher should be aware of the negative effect a lengthy, foreign text can have on some students, adults or children. Frequently, games, humour, visuals, puzzles, role play and other unusual approaches can motivate students' interest as well as providing opportunities for reflection and insight.

Ironically one way of stimulating interest is to withold the text and spend one or more lessons in the pre-reading stage building interest in and curiosity about characters, places, themes, and action by permitting only tantalizing glimpses of small selections from the text. These snippets must be carefully selected; they must stimulate curiosity, but not provide so much information that the need to read is removed. The pre-reading stage is important as it can whet the students' appetites to read; it can provide a *need* to read to complete an activity or confirm an idea; and it can persuade the students that as far as perception or hypothesis is concerned there are no right or wrong answers, only different ones.

Hypothesis is encouraged at the pre-reading stage because it is impossible for students to give a 'right' answer in traditional terms as none of them has read the text. The teacher must resist the temptation to intervene and confirm or disprove any hypothesis; this diminishes the need to read.

1 Anticipation through chapter titles

1.1 What happens?

Several Readers are written with the traditional chapter format. If these chapters are given titles, as opposed to numbers as a means of identification, then a variety of activities are available.

LITERARY AIM

Anticipation of plot

LEVEL

Elementary to Advanced

TIME

20–30 minutes

PREPARATION

None.

IN CLASS

1 Write the following chapter titles on the board so that there are no visual clues from the cover of the Reader. Make sure that there are no vocabulary problems.

Example 1
1 A Change of Plan
2 Beached
3 The sea
4 The forest
5 Build-up
6 Matsutan
7 Kimono
8 The Ipoh tree
9 The Key
10 Decision at five o'clock
11 Escape boat
12 The Wind from the Gods

Example 2
1 A Letter for Adam
2 Adam goes to Darpur
3 An Identity Card
4 No Photographs
5 Adam changes his money order

2 You should also supply the title of the Reader: in this case the first example is from *Hijacked* (OUP), and the second is from *Rich Man – Poor Man* (Heinemann). The first example is not so immediately accessible as the second, but it is intended for students of higher ability who have more language for hypothesis at their disposal.

3 Ask the students, in groups, to make suggestions and guesses about what the chapter titles could possibly have to do with the title of the Reader. They could even suggest a possible plot line. Do not at this stage tell any students whether they are right, wrong, or close to the truth with their hypotheses. You must try to encourage the students to guess without worrying whether their guesses are correct or not.

1.2 Spot the genre

LITERARY AIM	**Anticipation of plot and theme acknowledgement of different categories and styles of writing**
LEVEL	**Intermediate to Advanced**
TIME	**20–30 minutes**
PREPARATION	None.
IN CLASS	1 Before supplying the chapter titles, ask the students what different categories they know of for stories. They should come up with almost all of the following without too much prompting: romance, adventure, war, crime, detection, horror, historical, spying, science fiction, fairy tale, legend, travel, western.

They may come up with others. For any they do not know by name ask instead for examples of the type.

2 Now supply the students with the titles of the chapters and ask them which categories they think the Reader could fall into. Encourage them to suggest and justify as many as possible and do not tell them if they have guessed the specific category for the Reader concerned.

1.3 By any other name

LITERARY AIM	**Anticipation and hypothesis about plot and theme**
LEVEL	**Elementary to Advanced**
TIME	**20–30 minutes**
PREPARATION	None.
IN CLASS	1 Using the chapter titles in activity A1.1 from *Hijacked* (OUP) list them, in the correct order, on the blackboard.

2 Now write the following suggested book titles on the board:
– *Japanese Adventure*
– *A Journey by Boat*

  – *They Died for their Country*
  – *Hijacked*
  – *The Rain People*

3 Ask the students to work in groups and decide which of the suggested book titles would be the most suitable for the chapter titles. They must justify their choices based on the information they are extracting from the chapter titles, or the interpretation they are placing upon them.

1.4 I name this book

LITERARY AIM

Anticipation of plot and theme

LEVEL

Elementary to Advanced

TIME

15–25 minutes

PREPARATION

None.

IN CLASS

1 Write the following chapter titles on the blackboard. They are taken from *Don't Tell Me What To Do* (Heinemann):

  1 On My Own
  2 A Job with Masters
  3 Shirley
  4 The Swimming Pool
  5 My Bag is Searched
  6 Something Very Valuable
  7 Don't Tell Me What to Do
  8 An Argument
  9 A Lucky Escape
  10 Learning to Use the Scuba Suit
  11 A Man Called Lewis
  12 The Job Begins
  13 Inside *The Kular*
  14 Questions Are Answered

2 Divide the students into small groups and ask them to discuss each of the chapter titles and suggest a possible title for the Reader. They must try to justify their decisions.

3 At no time should you try to influence the groups in order to manipulate a choice which coincides with the actual title of the Reader. The right answer is *not* important. The students' responses to the chapter titles are what is being explored.

1.5 Once upon a title

LITERARY AIM	**Revision of familiar stories, anticipation and preconceptions of plot**
LEVEL	**Elementary to Advanced**
TIME	**20–25 minutes**
PREPARATION	None.
IN CLASS	This activity works well if it is a story which is fairly well known already, for example a fairy tale, or the story of a popular film.

1 Give the students the title of the Reader concerned, in this case *The Piper of Hamelin* (OUP) which is a fairly well-known story.

2 Ask them what they know about the story already. Then write the titles of the chapters on the blackboard, but not in the correct order, for example,

– 'Give Me My Money'
– The Mountain
– The Piper
– The Sad Town
– 'Come into the River for a Swim'
– The Rats of Hamelin
– A Different Tune

3 Ask the students to suggest an order.

1.6 Plot thickening

LITERARY AIM	**Anticipation of plot, hypothesis about theme and plot**
LEVEL	**Intermediate to Advanced**
TIME	**25–30 minutes**
PREPARATION	None.
IN CLASS	

1 Divide the class into groups. The number of groups should correspond to the number of chapters in the Reader you use.

2 Give each group a single, different chapter title. Tell the groups to treat the titles as if they were those of a complete Reader as opposed to merely a chapter. Ask them what they think the story of this new Reader might be?

3 When the entire class has suggested plots for each of the chapter titles help them to put the chapters in order.

4 As an optional extension to this activity ask for suggestions for a plot or story-line for the actual Reader from which they were taken.

1.7 What's in a name?

LITERARY AIM	To gauge emotional response to chapter titles; discuss preconceptions
LEVEL	Intermediate to Advanced
TIME	30–45 minutes
PREPARATION	None.
IN CLASS	**1** Write the chapter titles in random order on the blackboard and ask the students to arrange them in descending order according to how interesting they sound. They should be able to justify their choices, but there is no need for consensus. **2** As an optional exercise ask the students to decide which chapter title would make the best book title, and to explain why. Which would make a good LP title and why? Which would make a good name for a pop group and why? What do these titles suggest to them if the context is changed? Ask the students for other contexts in which any of these titles could be used.
COMMENT	This activity works best if students work alone first, then in pairs, and finally in larger groups before feeding the ideas back to the class as a whole. After reading has actually taken place a comparison can be made between their anticipations about the chapters and how they feel about what they have read.

2 Anticipation of plot

2.1 Read all about it

LITERARY AIM	Anticipation of plot, perception of clues and details, connecting ideas, imaginative discussion
LEVEL	Intermediate to Advanced
TIME	50–60 minutes

PREPARATION

Decide how many groups to divide your class into. Then make photocopies of the newspaper front page at the end of this activity. This example can be used with *The Thirty-Nine Steps* (Longman). Cut out each headline ready for distribution (one to each group), keeping back enough copies of the complete front page for distribution to each group later in the activity.

If you are using a different Reader from the one suggested and are therefore preparing your own materials, try not to make the headlines too obvious or there will not be any point in hypothesizing about the contents of the story. For example:

POLITICIAN MURDERED BY FRIEND

leaves very little to the imagination. Whereas,

ENGLAND MOURNS FOR MINISTER: FRIEND HELPING POLICE

is more cryptic and it allows the students to make several sensible yet imaginative guesses about what has been happening, without stating categorically what is in the news story (or the Reader).

WARM-UP

Find two or three genuine headlines to accompany simple and short news stories. Show the headlines to the students and ask them what they expect to read in the stories. Point out that the language of headlines is quite specialized and that certain rules are broken. If the students can recognize which rules are broken, so much the better. If not, draw attention to the absence of articles and use of present tense for past events, etc. Time taken at this stage will pay dividends later in the post-reading stage, if the newspaper format is to be used by the students as a summary technique for the same or another Reader.

IN CLASS

1 Each of the headlines can be used in a teacher-class discussion, or the different headlines can be given to different groups.

2 If you choose to divide the class into groups, distribute one headline to each group and ask the students to study their particular headline. When they have finished, ask each group to exchange their headline with that of another group.

3 When all the groups have seen all the headlines, allow the students time to exchange ideas about what might be in the accompanying article, from group to group.

4 Now show the class the newspaper front page with all the headlines in position. Until this point the class has not been told that all the headlines are linked in any way, or that they are concerned with one particular Reader.

5 Ask the students to try to make connections between the headlines. In order not to ruin the suspense, you should avoid a headline which reveals the final outcome. Pre-reading activities are meant to stimulate the students' curiosity, not to replace the Reader itself.

WEEKLY TIMES

1913 2d

'Dead' hero saves Parliament! Holds back time on Big Ben IS EUROPE SAFE?

Agent makes three. Triple Killer Search

Tragic loss!

Sir David Hamilton dies in Scottish home

Shooting in Scotland Hannay dead! Police close case

Hamilton Fiancé- Hopes for future happiness

39 steps Notebook code broken

BRITISH AGENT TOLD M.P. s OF PLOT

Lord Harkness *Murdered.* Parliament's loss doubled

NOTE: You may make photocopies of this for classroom use (but please note that copyright law does not normally permit multiple copying of published material).

2.2 It's all in the stars

LITERARY AIM   Anticipation of plot, perception of clues and details,
connecting ideas, imaginative discussion

LEVEL   Intermediate to Advanced

TIME   60 minutes

PREPARATION   1 Find a newspaper or magazine which includes astrological
predictions in English and prepare some simplified versions.

2 Prepare a summary of the Reader in three forecasts like the
examples at the end of this activity, which have been written using
the two main protagonists from *Hijacked* (OUP).

IN CLASS   1 Most students are familiar with the idea of foretelling the future.
A brief discussion at the start of the lesson will elicit from them
various methods of doing this including, probably, astrology.
Whether or not they actually believe in astrological predictions will
not affect the activity.

2 Distribute the samples of authentic horoscopes from magazines
and newspapers which are current for the day, week, or month of
the lesson. Ask the students if there is any connection between their
current reality and their current forecast. They may be prepared to
elaborate, but this is not necessary.

3 If possible find out the signs of one or two people whom you
know will interest your students, for example, famous celebrities
such as pop singers, political figures, or sports personalities. Ask
how their current forecast would affect these celebrities if they
believed in astrology. Is it a good time for a summit meeting, for
example, or for making a new record, or playing an important
football match?

4 Then, as an optional extra, ask the students to suggest what
might have been in a forecast written in the past for a famous
historical figure on a particular day. What was Julius Caesar's
forecast on the day he was murdered? What was Christopher
Columbus' forecast on the day that he discovered America? The
students should be reminded that the language of horoscopes is
always general and vague.

5 Now begin to introduce the summary of the Reader you have
selected. The summary should be written in the form of three
parallel forecasts for the two main protagonists. These forecasts
must be written by you at the pre-reading stage, but the students
themselves can summarize another Reader in this way after
reading. The preparation of these forecasts is not difficult, but the
language must be at the right level, and the style and register should
appear as authentic as possible.

6 The first forecast should deal with the beginning of the plot, the second with some major turning point which affects both protagonists, and the third with the eventual outcome. In keeping with the vagueness of authentic forecasts no specific facts are given.

7 Distribute the forecasts in stages with the students working in groups of four or five. In the example provided, the students would receive the 5 January forecast first. At this stage do not tell them that there is any relationship between the two people. Tell the class that these two forecasts were extremely accurate. So what sorts of experiences could a Leo and an Aquarian have had on this day? One side of the class can work on Leo and the other on Aquarius, if preferred.

8 Introduce the 6 and 10 January forecasts in the same way, and after the third forecast has been distributed ask the students to try to link the three forecasts with some sort of narrative thread.

9 Next, allow the students to see all six forecasts and give them some very basic information about the characters, for example, age, nationality, and job. In this example they would be told that Leo is a 16-year-old English schoolboy and that Aquarius is a former university student from Japan who is in his twenties. How does this knowledge affect their interpretations?

10 Next, tell them under what circumstances the two protagonists will meet and how they will be affected. These two characters will meet under violent conditions and will learn to hate each other. How does this knowledge affect the students' interpretations?

11 Finally, tell the students the title of the book in which these two characters will meet and ask again how this affects their interpretations. As previously stated this example is produced for the Reader *Hijacked* (OUP).

COMMENT

During all of the above stages it is essential that you give the groups sufficient time to reflect on the information and to adjust their response to it as each new layer of information is added. It is not essential that any group foretells with a hundred per cent accuracy the plot and the relationship between the two characters. Allow them to submit their ideas without providing them with the right answer. Then, the only way the students can find out if their guesses were correct is to read the book.

LEO 5 January	LEO 6 January	LEO 10 January
Avoid long journeys today. Your ambition is almost achieved, but be prepared for an unexpected problem. Appearances can be deceptive. Remember loved ones and be patient. A day of surprises.	Be prepared to think and act quickly today. You may get out of one problem and into another. You will get a chance to show talent and courage today, but be prepared for a violent disagreement with a new acquaintance. Take care of your health, people are depending on you.	A day for physical courage. Take the advice of those with more experience. A situation which has been troubling you is finally resolved. Your loved ones are worried so try to remember them. Your ambition is closer to being fulfilled. It is a good day for travelling.

AQUARIUS 5 January	AQUARIUS 6 January	AQUARIUS 10 January
You are a dreamer, but today is a day when your dreams could come true. You may have to lie to get what you want. A good day for travelling, but delays are to be expected. Try to control your violent nature and bad temper.	A friend you were relying on has failed to do as you asked and you are kept waiting. Try not to get too impatient or you may do something you regret. People in authority stop you getting everything you want today. Wait. A good friend is trying to contact you.	Not a good day for those interested in political ideals. Your plans receive a major set-back. Avoid water if you can. People in authority have a good right to be angry with you and you should stay calm if you want to avoid an embarrassing end to all your present hopes.

NOTE: You may make photocopies of this for classroom use (but please note that copyright law does not normally permit multiple copying of published material).

2.3 Take a letter

LITERARY AIM

Anticipation of plot and the role of characters within that plot, perception of clues and details, connecting of ideas, imaginative discussion

LEVEL

Elementary to Advanced

TIME

60 minutes minimum

PREPARATION

If the text of the Reader includes several notes or letters written by one or more of the characters these letters can be extracted from the text to provide a pre-reading problem-solving activity. The letters should not be presented in any particular order and no comment should be provided by you. The examples at the end of this activity are taken from *Space Affair* (OUP).

IN CLASS

1 Divide the students into three groups and give each group a different letter. Ask them to hypothesize as to what the story is about and what type of story it might be. Explain that the letters are linked and are written by two people.

2 Now ask the students, in their groups, to discuss the following specific points:

– Do any of the characters reveal anything about themselves?
– What seems to be the main problem?
– Why do the letters appear to have been written in each case?
– What are the relationships between the writer of each letter and the recipient?

3 You may need to help out with vocabulary concerning the specific points. Make sure all the students understand before they begin their discussions.

4 Give the groups sufficient time to discuss the points thoroughly. Then ask all the students to form three new groups. Each member of the new groups tells the other members what his or her letter was about.

5 Finally, having shared all their information, ask the groups to try to decide what the story is about.

COMMENT

This technique can also provide a way in for unsimplified texts too, including Cambridge Local Examination Prescribed Texts, such as Patricia Highsmith's detective novel *The Talented Mr Ripley*, which is peppered with notes and letters which the students enjoyed reading and analysing before they looked at the text itself. The activity usually works well with any detective or espionage story as the students share the atmosphere of mystery.

Dear Alpha 3461,
Can I call you 61? Or can I call you by your real name? I'm Gareth Palmer, and I'm a garden technician. I'm 26, and I come from London in the United European District on Earth. This is my first space trip, and I'm going to stay on Orelia Five, so it's probably my last space trip, too. I don't know why I want to know about you, but I do. But I don't want you to do anything dangerous. You know what happens to people who break the rules. Be careful!
Very best wishes,
Gareth

Dear Beta 4297,
Thank you for finding my earring. And thank you for the flower. You mustn't do anything like that again. It's dangerous for you! I've often wondered about you. I don't know anything about you. I know you're a man. You didn't clean the sink very well after you shaved, and the cleaners are not very careful in this area of the ship. Well, we'll meet on Orelia Five. Until then, good luck!
Best wishes,
Alpha 3461

Dear Programmer,
I am interested in the history of television on Centauri.
Your program talks about television in 2298. I saw a
programme from Centauri once. It was a very old one.
I saw it on an old video. It was called *I love you too*.
When was that programme made? Please reply.
Yours,
Garden technician, Beta 4297

2.4 Documentaries

LITERARY AIM

Anticipation of plot, connecting ideas, ability to perceive and respond to small details, imaginative story-telling

LEVEL

Intermediate to Advanced

TIME

60 minutes

PREPARATION

Prepare a visual summary of all the possible documents which could have contributed to the story line of the Reader. This is not so complicated as it sounds as documents can include anything from newspaper headlines of incidents which would merit news coverage, to humble bus tickets which would denote that a journey had taken place. Documents can include: obituaries, announcements of births, wedding banns, 'for sale' notices, menus and bills, bus and train tickets and time-tables, maps and charts, shopping lists, grafitti, notices and posters, diary entries, prescriptions, warning signs, memos, book covers, greeting cards, tombstones, et al.

The documents should relate to, or be associated with a specific incident in the Reader, but they may not be mentioned explicitly. For example, the bus ticket itself may not be mentioned, but if a journey by bus took place there must have been a ticket, and vice versa.

No great artistic talent is required to produce the documents as the majority of them are found within the rectangular boundaries of pieces of paper, but there should be an air of authenticity about them. They do not have to be drawn to scale, but they are more effective if they are. If you take a bit of trouble with this activity at this stage then there will be less confusion when the students try to produce their own documentary summaries as a post-reading activity for another Reader. If the documents are drawn they should be cut up separately so that the students can play around with the order and not be influenced by the order in which the documents are presented to them. The examples at the end of this activity have been designed to accompany *Animal Farm* (Longman).

IN CLASS

1 Divide the class into groups and give each group the collection of documents.

2 Allow them time to study all the documents, and to identify what sort of a document is which, for example, a poster, a song sheet, etc. Then ask what each document usually signifies: a poster is usually giving information to a large number; a flag usually suggests a country or territory and patriotism.

3 When all the documents have been identified and reasons for their existence have been suggested, ask the students to arrange the documents in an order which tells a story – any story they care to invent, but all the documents must be included.

4 Finally, the ideas for the stories are shared with the entire class.

F

G
Newsagent
Please deliver
'Daily Mail'
to Animal Farm.
Charge to account

H
BEASTS of ENGLAND
Lyrics by Old Major

I
☆ INVITATION ☆
You are invited to a party
at Animal Farm
Card-playing, drinks
and supper
Chez-nous Napoleon   RSVP

J

THE SEVEN COMMANDMENTS

1. Whatever goes on two legs is an enemy.
2. Whatever goes on four legs or has wings is a friend.
3. No animal shall wear clothes.
4. No animal shall sleep in a bed.
5. No animal shall drink alcohol.
6. No animal shall kill any other animal.
7. All animals are equal.

K
IN MEMORIAM
TO WHOM IT MAY CONCERN
MR. G. JONES FORMERLY OF
MANOR FARM DIED OF LIVER
DISEASE IN ST. MARKS HOME
FOR DISTRESSED GENTLEFOLK
EARLY THIS MORNING.

L

M
BAC
Learn to read and write

2.5 Cover story

LITERARY AIM

Anticipation of plot, response to visual stimuli representing text

LEVEL

Intermediate to Advanced

TIME

60 minutes minimum

PREPARATION

If the Reader which you, or your students have selected is available in more than one form or edition, it is extremely useful to obtain as many versions of the cover illustrations as possible. For example a visit to only two bookshops yielded six different covers for the story of *Animal Farm*. (See the illustrations at the end of this activity which are published by Heinemann, Longman and Penguin.) You must also prepare topic 'bubbles' which surround the various versions of the covers to stimulate discussion.

IN CLASS

1 Introduce the idea of judging a book by its cover to your students and find out how easily influenced they are by cover artwork. Ask the following questions:
– What do your students think publishers are aiming to do when they design a cover?
– How important is the lettering?
– Do different styles of lettering suggest different things?
– When they look at a jacket design do the students expect to learn about the plot of the book or more about its theme?

2 The second stage of the lesson can be done, optionally, as a role play, but not necessarily. Suggest that your students try to put themselves in the frame of publishers who are trying to decide on the cover for their next publication, in this case *Animal Farm*.

3 Divide the students into groups. Distribute the different versions of the covers with questions attached which they must take into account. Encourage them to make notes. Remind the students that the cover must be memorable.

4 Allow each group time to see each cover in turn and consider the questions until they are once more faced with the cover with which they started.

5 Ask for feedback from each group. This can start off along the lines of 'I like' or 'I don't like'. They should be asked to justify all subjective comments.

6 Then ask the students how much they have learnt about the plot or the theme from the covers. These ideas can be transferred to the blackboard under the headings 'I think' and 'I know'.

7 Next, introduce the concept of minority audiences and ask which cover they would choose for the following various groups of readers:
– children and adolescents
– those with artistic talents

– romantic females
– unenthusiastic readers who prefer video
– political activists.

At all stages ask them for justification.

8 Finally, display all the covers so that all groups can see them and ask them to chose the cover which will have the widest appeal and, therefore, sell the most copies. The groups should not confer with each other, but there should be discussion within each group. Ask the groups to make their recommendations on memos which provide the opportunity for a form of guided writing.

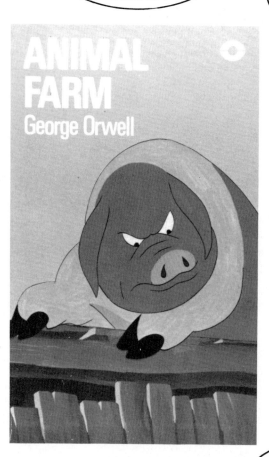

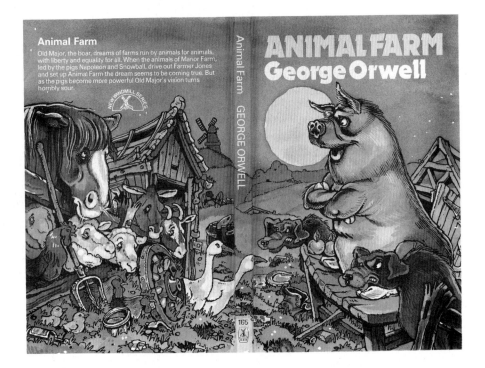

MEMORANDUM
_____

FROM: Publicity Department
TO: Editorial Department
RE: Choice of Cover
_____

We recommend that you choose cover .... because ....
....
....
....

2.6 Picture hypothesis

LITERARY AIM

Perception of connecting details and clues found in visual information usually accompanying text

LEVEL

Elementary to Advanced

TIME

45–60 minutes

INTRODUCTION

Most of us have been in the position of standing outside a cinema trying to make sense of the stills on display which are there to help us anticipate the film we are about to see. Usually, in that situation, we have the title of the film to help us, but this activity is more effective in the classroom if the title of the Reader is withheld from the students.

The students could easily treat the illustrations you select as if they were stills from a film if this would enable them to be more imaginative in their responses.

PREPARATION

Select four or five illustrations from the Reader of your choice. If possible mount the originals on card so that all textual clues are removed. There should be no indication of the order in which they are found in the Reader, so page numbers should also be removed. For example, look at the illustrations at the end of this activity which have been taken from *Rich Man-Poor Man* (Heinemann).

IN CLASS

1 Divide the class into groups of four or five. Each group has a set of the pictures.

2 Write the following points on the blackboard, and ask the students to come to some decisions concerning them:

– What do we learn about the period of time in which this story takes place? How do people dress, act, live, spend their free time?
– What relationships are evident in the pictures, for example, are they husband and wife, parent and child? Do these people like each other? Does any one of them have authority over any of the others?
– What seems to be happening in each picture? How do the people involved seem to feel about what is happening? Is there a feeling of fear, romance, excitement or anything else?
– Arrange the pictures to tell a brief story. Give your picture story a title. If you had to select only one of the illustrations to be used in an advertising campaign to sell your story which one would it be?

3 When you are certain that each group has its ideas clearly established then the groups can exchange opinions and story ideas. Do not tell any group that they are right or close to the actual plot of the Reader. Instead encourage them to be imaginative in their discussions.

COMMENT _____ This activity is made even more interesting and fruitful if each group has a different set of five pictures from the Reader.

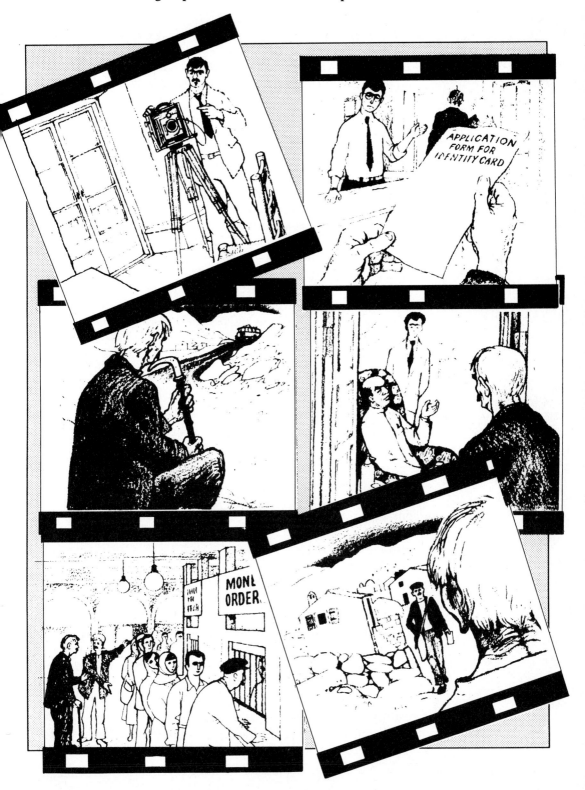

3 Thematic anticipation

3.1 A picture equals a thousand words

LITERARY AIM Perception of visual details inspired by text, ability to respond subjectively to prompts and to perceive thematic possibilities

LEVEL Elementary to Advanced

TIME 45 minutes

PREPARATION Choose a picture from the Reader which represents its theme or shows a key character or event. 'Theme' here and elsewhere, means a recurrent or important idea in the book. For this activity we have used *Tales from the Arabian Nights* (OUP). (See the illustration at the end of this activity.) If you use another Reader separate the picture from the text so that there are no textual clues to distract the students. The activity works even better if the students do not know the title of the Reader they are to begin work on. The picture is then surrounded with questions for which there are no right or wrong answers, only different ones. The object of the exercise is not to guess accurately what is going on in the picture, but to hypothesize about and discuss all the different possibilities for such a picture.

IN CLASS 1 This activity works best in pairs. Try to have one illustration for each pair if possible. Pairs can either answer alternate questions and work in a clockwise direction around the illustration, or they choose questions at random according to the amount of interest generated.

2 When asking the students to describe the picture suggest to them that their description should begin with the items which they consider to be the least important, and build up to the most important. You should stress that these are different for every student and, therefore, the descriptions will be slightly different in every case.

3 Encourage your students to justify any comments they make to each other at this stage in any way they can. For example, when they are asked to suggest a title for their picture they should try to explain the reasons for their choice and not assume that their choice is self-explanatory.

4 Encourage them to be as imaginative as possible with their answers and remind them that they will not be penalized for wrong guesses.

5 When they are asked to list words which they associate with the picture ask them not to list merely the nouns which they can see. You may have to explain the idea of association.

6 After the pairs have discussed all the topics surrounding the picture ask each pair to share their response with the whole class.

COMMENT

When devising exercises like this try to give equal weight to all elements of the picture, whether or not they carry equal weight in the story itself. For instance, when using the example here, it does not really matter to the story what the man in the striped outfit has in his bag, but by asking for an opinion on this you shift the emphasis away from the more predictable topics, and encourage the students to hypothesize more inventively, as well as reinforcing the idea that in creative work very little is not deliberate. Avoid closed questions such as those asking for specific vocabulary items.

3.2 Thematic montage

LITERARY AIM

Anticipation of and response to theme

LEVEL

Elementary to Advanced

TIME

60 minutes minimum

PREPARATION

Either you or your students need to collect together a bank of resource materials such as English magazines and newspapers for the montages. If you ask your students to supply the material make sure you warn them well in advance of the lesson. Bring to the class enough large pieces of stiff card or paper (A3 size) to display the finished montage work.

IN CLASS

1 Divide the class into groups and supply each group with a large piece of card.

2 Tell them the theme of their montage which is also the theme, or one of the possible themes of the Reader. You can, if you wish, use one of these examples:

Themes for montage	Titles of Readers
Rebellion or power	*Animal Farm*
Terrorism or heroism	*Hijacked*
Patriotism	*The Thirty-Nine Steps*
Parent and child	*Silas Marner*

3 At this stage, the students are not required to know anything about the title or contents of the Reader itself.

4 Supply each group with a pile of magazines and newspapers. This does not have to be extensive as the groups can exchange.

5 Tell each group that the ingredients of their montage must include as many of the following as possible, which must all be linked to the theme or idea given to them by you:
- 10 key words or phrases suggested by the group
- 5 news headlines
- 5 extracts from news stories or articles
- 2 cartoons
- 1 poem or extract from a poem
- 1 extract from a song
- 2 song titles
- 2 slogans suitable for printing on to tee-shirts
- 2 film titles

plus any pictures they can find related to the theme.

6 Ask them to arrange their pictures on their piece of card to make maximum visual and emotional impact. The research for the ingredients can be done at home if you cannot justify the time in class. The discussion about the ingredients and the subsequent layout and display should be done in class.

7 Monitor the groups and at regular intervals ask why a certain item is being included. On their completion each montage should be displayed. You can call upon any of the groups to explain the reasons for any ingredients in their montage.

8 The Reader, when it is finally read, can supply even more components. As the students encounter episodes or quotations which echo or reflect the theme of the montage they can be noted down and added to the montage as a sort of frame or border around it. Make sure that the students suggest these quotations, not you.

COMMENT

A project does not necessarily have to come *after* a reading. Instead the Reader can form the climax of a project, and the project can also serve as a pre-reading or warm-up exercise.

4 Character anticipation

4.1 If the face fits

LITERARY AIM

Anticipation of character, perception of and response to details from text

LEVEL

Intermediate to Advanced

TIME

60 minutes minimum

INTRODUCTION

With increasing frequency Readers, especially those at the 1000 headword level, have no illustrations. Students are becoming increasingly visually orientated, perhaps because of the rise in the popularity of TV and video, and one way of capitalizing on this is to ask them to tap the visual response which they may not realize they have formed after exposure to only small parts of the text.

PREPARATION

To enable the students to do this you must prepare diagrams for the characters to be considered. The examples provided with this activity are for three of the eleven characters in *Animal Farm* (Longman). The information on the diagrams comes from the Reader itself. You should not add any extra subjective information. The information need not be provided in diagram form, but this method of presentation means that the students can start at any point they wish on the diagram and move in any direction. You should also find, or prepare a selection of at least thirty pictures of different types of people. A list of adjectives is provided at the end of this activity and you may make copies for each pair or group of students. This list can be used with any Reader.

IN CLASS

1 It is more useful and economical in terms of time to divide the class into groups or pairs. Each pair or group will work on a different character from the Reader. The pairs or groups can pool their information at a later stage.

2 Distribute copies of the diagrams (one to each pair or group), plus a copy of the adjective list.

3 After they have read the information ask the students to tick the sample adjective list. They tick the adjectives which they feel apply to the character they are working on based only on the information found in the diagrams. They should be prepared to explain why they have chosen these characteristics.

4 Next, provide each pair or group with as many pictures of people as possible. The selection should include young and old, male and female, fat and thin, good- and bad-humoured. Ask each pair or group to choose a picture to accompany all the information they have about their character. The pictures should be numbered for ease of identification.

5 Ask each group to write a brief explanation of why they chose that particular picture. What do they think the picture reveals of the character as shown in the initial diagram?

6 Circulate all the pictures and explanations and/or pin them on the wall. Ask the class to say whether or not they agree with the choices made and give their reasons.

VARIATION

As an alternative to you providing the pictures for the students to select from, allow them to bring to the following lesson one picture each of their own choice. Each group will then have three or four pictures to consider for the character they are working on.

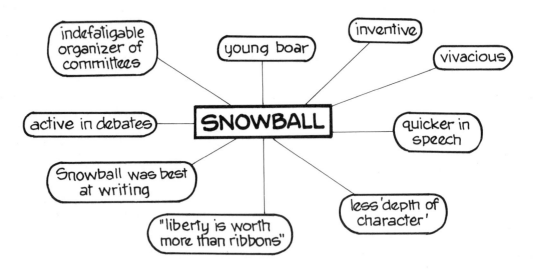

Now that you have some idea of the character that your group has been looking at, check off on the list below the adjectives that you would choose to describe this character.

☐ Intelligent   ☐ Mean
☐ Stupid   ☐ Dark
☐ Old   ☐ Fair
☐ Young   ☐ Fat
☐ Male   ☐ Thin
☐ Female   ☐ Energetic
☐ Articulate   ☐ Lazy
☐ Quiet   ☐ Good-humoured
☐ Talkative   ☐ Humourless
☐ Secretive   ☐ Cynical
☐ Vain   ☐ Naïve
☐ Humble   ☐ Slow moving
☐ A leader   ☐ Agile
☐ A follower   ☐ Direct in movement
☐ Honest   ☐ Meandering in movement
☐ Dishonest   ☐ Strong
☐ Trustworthy   ☐ Weak
☐ Generous   ☐ Apathetic

4.2 Dear Marj

LITERARY AIM   **Anticipation of character and relationships. Subjective perception of and response to details from the text**

LEVEL   **Elementary to Advanced**

TIME   **60 minutes**

INTRODUCTION

This pre-reading activity encourages the students to focus on the main dilemma or problem facing the characters in the Readers. The same problem is looked at from as many points of view as possible. This enables the students to identify more closely with the characters and to see the relevance of the theme to their own lives.

PREPARATION

You will need to create the letters which have been supposedly written by the characters concerned to the magazine problem page. Any pains taken by you now will ensure greater success at a later stage when the students, after reading another book, can produce their own problem letters.

First, make a list of all the main characters and then the secondary characters within the framework of the Reader. Try to imagine how the problem would be viewed from their point of view. They may not share the same problem, but each character will have something which is troubling them. For example, in the story of 'Cinderella' poor Cinder's problem would be the treatment she receives from her step-sisters. The step-sisters themselves would be complaining about the lazy girl who does nothing around the house and makes them feel angry because she is so much more beautiful than they are. The father's problem would be his domineering second wife, while Prince Charming would worry about the difficulty of meeting anyone who isn't interested in his money and position as heir to the throne. Most stories, from fairy tales to the classics, lend themselves easily to this shift of focus. Examples of the types of letters needed appear at the end of this activity, and they can be used with *The Stranger* (Heinemann). You may make copies of the letters for classroom use.

IN CLASS

1 The aim of this activity is not only to hypothesize over the relationships between the people who have written these letters, but also to suggest advice which could help to solve these problems. It is, therefore, not a good idea to let the whole class see all the letters simultaneously. Instead, divide the class into groups, one group for each problem letter.

2 The groups must, first of all, identify what the problem is and then offer the character advice. At this stage the students are not aware of the connection between all the letters.

3 Allow the groups of students time to finish their work on individual letters and then have a 'case conference' at which each group presents a brief summary of the problem they have been dealing with and the advice they are going to offer through their magazine pages.

4 When all the problems have been described and the characters have received a letter of reply and some advice, ask the class to suggest how these characters are interlinked, and also what the students think will happen to these characters if they do not follow the advice which they have just received.

Dear Marj,

My problem is that I don't know whether to mind my own business, or not. I live in a small village. We all know and care about each other. Recently, a young man entered our lives. He has opened up a small shop. At first I didn't want this shop, and I argued very loudly against it. Now the shop is doing well and it sells a lot of my garden flowers to the tourists. I bought a big new TV with the money. The trouble is that I think this new man is causing problems for a young couple, Pete and Anna. They are going to get married, but I know that Anna has been to London for the weekend with the stranger. I can't talk to her. She looks ill and pale. I also do not want to upset our shopkeeper because I enjoy the money I get for my flowers. Should I just keep quiet?

Neighbour

Dear Marj,

I am no longer as young as I was, but they say I am still beautiful. My talent as an actress is still there, but the parts are going to younger women. There is a part in a new film that I want very much. I have tried everything to get it, but I feel certain they will give it to a younger actress. The worry is spoiling my health and I am getting desperate. What can I do to make sure that I get this part?

G.G

Dear Marj,

I am seventeen and engaged to marry a boy from our village. Recently, I have become very attracted to my boss who is much older and richer than my boyfriend. My boss takes me out, buys me new clothes and takes me away on trips. My boyfriend only bothers about football and never buys me any presents. I don't know what to do. My boss isn't from our village and he has a lot of strange business that I know nothing about. When I ask him questions he gets very angry. I have no friends I can talk to about this. What should I do?

Confused

Dear Marj,

I am from a small village where I have lived all my life. I am very happy there. I have a lovely girlfriend and lots of friends. I play football every Saturday. Unfortunately, jobs are not very good in the village and my girlfriend and I will have to save very hard if we want to get married next year. I don't know if I should leave the village for a year and try to get a better job. If I go my girlfriend might change her mind about me and meet someone else. She already seems a bit different now she is working in the village shop. I think she is attracted to her boss. Should I leave the village and try another job, or will I lose my girlfriend?

Worried

NOTE: You may make photocopies of this for classroom use (but please note that copyright law does not normally permit multiple copying of published material).

4.3 Patchwork

LITERARY AIM	Anticipation of character and relationships. Subjective response to details from text
LEVEL	Intermediate to Advanced
TIME	45–60 minutes

INTRODUCTION Students can be disappointed if a Reader does not contain enough 'action' by their standards. Their disappointment might be lessened if they received more help in developing an appreciation of characterization. If a story deals more with character than with incident you should take the opportunity to ask the students to look more closely at character by extracting small snippets of text which deal predominantly with this and making the activity more of a problem-solving one. Each snippet of text should imply something about the characters involved without the benefit of a full context. There are usually enough clues in very small pieces of text for the students to pick up certain implications.

PREPARATION The example at the end of this activity is from 'The Doll's House', *Outstanding Short Stories* (Longman).

IN CLASS 1 Divide the students into groups of three or four.

2 Ask them to read the page about the Burnell family without conferring, but as they read they should make notes about the members of this family. If the students are not confident enough to make their own notes freely then you can ask them to complete any of the following sentences:

I like the way . . .
I don't like the way . . .
I think . . .
I do not think that . . .
I am unhappy about . . .
I am pleased about . . .
I am confused about . . .

3 Make it clear to the students that they are 'reading between the lines' and looking at what each quotation reveals, or suggests, rather than what it means literally.

4 Allow only a few minutes for this introductory stage, or the responses will become less spontaneous.

5 Ask the students to exchange information with the other members of their group. They can expand their notes at this stage as they listen.

6 Next, ask the entire class to report back on their findings, or else group members can visit other groups to find out what the others have thought. The notes should be extended again if possible.

7 Now carry out the same exercise with the information on the Kelvey family.

8 When both patchworks have been analysed and the students feel that they have shared their responses, give each group a list of questions to discuss which have subjective answers, for example:

– Are the families different in any important ways?
– Which family would you prefer to be part of? Why?
– Which family would you like to visit?

- Is either of these families happy?
- How is each family treated by others?
- If you were a small girl which of these children would you choose as a friend?
- Which sister/sister relationship is closer?
- If you could give a present to one of these families what would it be?
- What single piece of advice would you give to each family?
- Describe the favourite toy of each family.
- What would each family do if they found £5?
- If you could give a present to each of these families what would it be?

Below you will see a 'patchwork' of bits and pieces about the Burnell family. Listen carefully to the teacher's instructions.

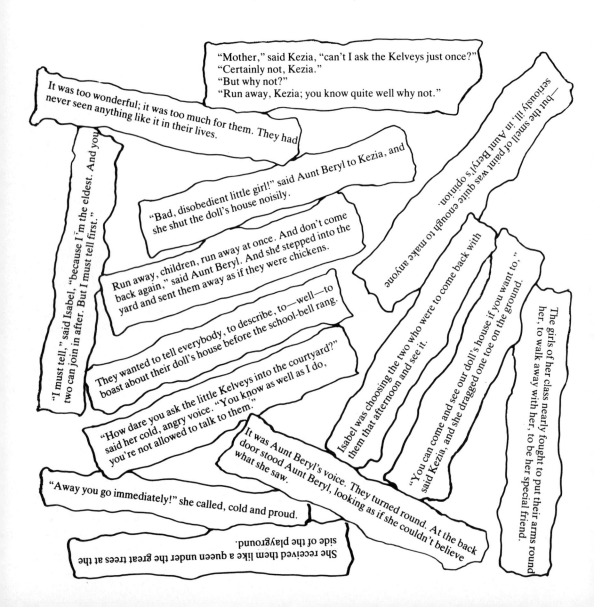

"Mother," said Kezia, "can't I ask the Kelveys just once?"
"Certainly not, Kezia."
"But why not?"
"Run away, Kezia; you know quite well why not."

It was too wonderful; it was too much for them. They had never seen anything like it in their lives.

—but the smell of paint was quite enough to make anyone seriously ill, in Aunt Beryl's opinion.

"I must tell," said Isabel, "because I'm the eldest. And you two can join in after. But I must tell first."

"Bad, disobedient little girl!" said Aunt Beryl to Kezia, and she shut the doll's house noisily.

Run away, children, run away at once. And don't come back again," said Aunt Beryl. And she stepped into the yard and sent them away as if they were chickens.

They wanted to tell everybody, to describe, to—well—to boast about their doll's house before the school-bell rang.

"How dare you ask the little Kelveys into the courtyard?" said her cold, angry voice. "You know as well as I do, you're not allowed to talk to them."

Isabel was choosing the two who were to come back with her, to walk away with her, to be her special friend.

The girls of her class nearly fought to put their arms round her, to walk away with her, to be her special friend.

"You can come and see our doll's house if you want to," said Kezia, and she dragged one toe on the ground.

Isabel was choosing the two who were to come back with them that afternoon and see it.

"Away you go immediately!" she called, cold and proud.

It was Aunt Beryl's voice. They turned round. At the back door stood Aunt Beryl, looking as if she couldn't believe what she saw.

She received them like a queen under the great trees at the side of the playground.

Below you will see a 'patchwork' of bits and pieces about the Kelvey family. Follow the teacher's instructions.

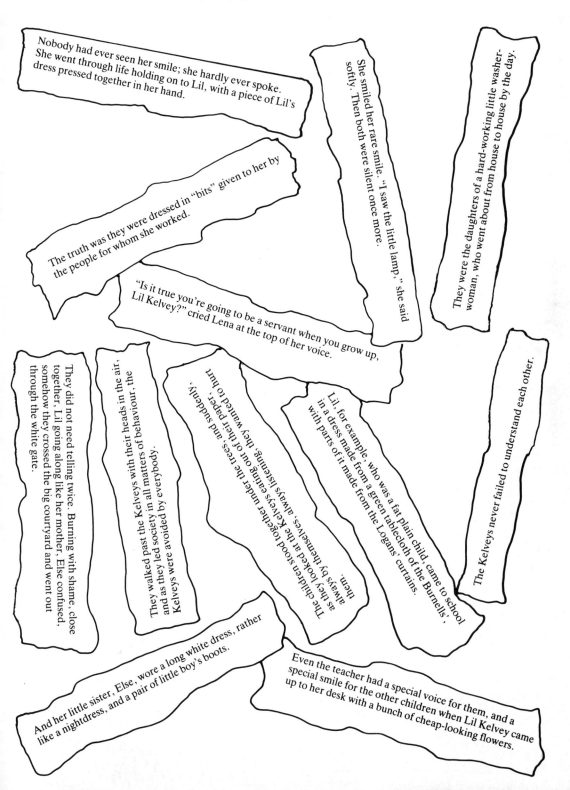

Nobody had ever seen her smile; she hardly ever spoke. She went through life holding on to Lil, with a piece of Lil's dress pressed together in her hand.

She smiled her rare smile. "I saw the little lamp," she said softly. Then both were silent once more.

They were the daughters of a hard-working little washer-woman, who went about from house to house by the day.

The truth was they were dressed in "bits" given to her by the people for whom she worked.

"Is it true you're going to be a servant when you grow up, Lil Kelvey?" cried Lena at the top of her voice.

They did not need telling twice. Burning with shame, close together, Lil going along like her mother, Else confused, somehow they crossed the big courtyard and went out through the white gate.

They walked past the Kelveys with their heads in the air, and as they led society in all matters of behaviour, the Kelveys were avoided by everybody.

The children stood together under the trees, and suddenly, as they looked at the Kelveys eating out of their paper, always by themselves, always listening, they wanted to hurt them.

Lil, for example, who was a fat plain child, came to school in a dress made from a green tablecloth of the Burnells', with parts of it made from the Logans' curtains.

The Kelveys never failed to understand each other.

And her little sister, Else, wore a long white dress, rather like a nightdress, and a pair of little boy's boots.

Even the teacher had a special voice for them, and a special smile for the other children when Lil Kelvey came up to her desk with a bunch of cheap-looking flowers.

5 Setting anticipation

5.1 Know your place!

LITERARY AIM **Awareness of setting and possible influence of setting upon character and action (and vice versa)**

LEVEL **Elementary to Advanced**

TIME **45–60 minutes**

INTRODUCTION Sometimes the location in which a story is set plays an integral part in the story itself. We are all used to this idea in more literary texts, but it also applies to simplified Readers. Setting, and a character's response to it can influence the pattern of subsequent events. If the students are to understand why a character is responding in a certain way, they must be given the opportunity to respond to all the hints and suggestions, implicit and explicit, which the author has included, and which should be actively affecting their responses to setting.

PREPARATION One way of doing this is through the patchwork technique. You should prepare a single page which is covered with single words or short phrases from the Reader which tell the students about the setting. These should be a mixture of facts and opinions, implicit and explicit comments. Arrange the comments on the page so that the student does not feel that there is a special place to start, nor a special order in which to read the pieces. The patchwork, given as an example is taken from *The Stranger* (Heinemann).

IN CLASS **Part one**
1 Divide the class into pairs or groups.

2 Give each pair or group a copy of the patchwork.

3 Allow the students ample time to read all the extracts.

4 Then ask them to categorize the extracts under the headings 'I know' and 'I think'. Our patchwork example would produce the following lists:

I Know	I Think
It is not a new town.	*It sounds attractive.*
It has a church.	*This may be a very religious place.*
It has no cinema.	*There's not much for young people.*
There is no work for young people.	*Perhaps old people are retired.*
It seems a friendly place.	*People are very curious.*
There are no shops and it is quiet and peaceful.	

The students should not simply copy the words down from the patchwork, but should try to make some comment or deduction.

5 The activity should have a limited time span or it will become very laboured. After, perhaps, only ten minutes, you should encourage the groups to exchange their information. This can be done by sending one member from each group on a circular tour of all the other groups.

Part two

6 When all the groups have heard each others' opinions ask them to write the name of the place vertically, letter by letter. In this case the place would be called w – o – o – d – e – n – d.

7 Give them time to think about the task which involves them providing ideas and/or vocabulary which reflects their response to this place. The ideas or vocabulary must begin with the letter of the line concerned. You can make dictionaries available to the students, if you wish. You may also have to provide an example of the sort of thing wanted. This can best be achieved with an example of your responses to either your home town or the town where you are teaching, for example:

A *Agamemnon, Ancient, Archeology, Acropolis*
T *Too much Traffic, Too many Tourists*
H *Hot Hellish Hotels, Hooting Horns*
E *Endurance is Essential, Exciting*
N *Noise, Nephos★*
S *Sunshine, Syrtaki, Souvlaki, Souvenirs*

★ word for the pollution cloud which hangs over the city.

So the town of Woodend could yield, for example:

W *Warm Words and Welcomes but no Work*
O *Opportunities for Optimists*
O *Old but Original*
D *Delightful but Dull*
E *Entertainment Elsewhere, Escape!*
N *Nice Normal Neighbours*
D *Depressing . . . Dangerous!*

IN A LATER CLASS

Part three: optional extension
Ask the students how they would feel living or being on holiday in the place which is receiving their attention. Ask them to send a postcard from the place concerned telling a friend what they have seen and done and how they feel about the place.

IN A LATER CLASS

Part four: optional extension (This type of rewriting exercise was first demonstrated to me by Dr Ronald Carter.)
After a brief discussion about the role of an estate agent and the sort of literature he produces to sell houses, ask the students to produce a 'For Sale' advertisement for a property in the place under consideration. This will involve the students playing down the negative sides of the place and accentuating the positive sides. Ask them also to discuss among themselves what sort of a person such a property would appeal to. The following is an example of the type of advertisement needed:

FOR SALE

Attractive village house, built on the corner of Main Street and Church Lane, in quiet, historic village of Woodend, opposite the beautiful village church. The house has been empty for several months and the windows and roof need repairs. The village of Woodend has a small shop selling bread, cakes, flowers and paintings. In the summer many tourists come to visit the village. There is a small school for young children and it also has a local doctor. In the centre of the village is the village hall which is a popular meeting place for the community. A regular bus service links Woodend to the nearby town of Lidney. In Lidney there are dress shops, cinemas, restaurants and plenty of jobs. Lidney also has a station with trains to Paddington Station in London.

FINAL STAGE   Ask the students to hypothesize what sort of a story they think will take place in a setting like the one they have considered.

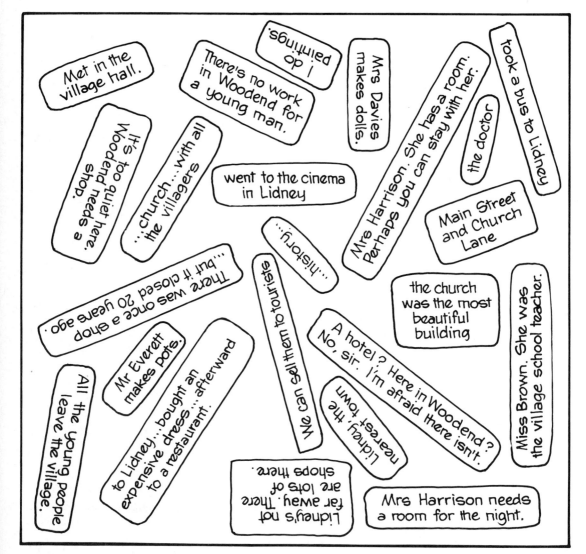

6 Background information

6.1 Writer's world

LITERARY AIM

Awareness of author's influences and anticipation of possible effects on text

LEVEL

Upper Intermediate to Advanced

TIME

120 minutes minimum

INTRODUCTION

Occasionally, with older and more academically-minded students especially, an interest in the author can trigger an interest in the Reader. One way of stimulating such an interest is to provide the opportunity to respond to selected biographical information. This does not mean a list of biographical data, as seldom, if ever, does this encourage either an awareness of the impact of such events upon the writer or any personal response from the students. The following activity allows the students to 'play around' with the chronological information and make it their own.

PREPARATION

By using encyclopaedias or other reference books create a 'cloudscape' of information about the author of the Reader you or your students have chosen. The example provided at the end of this activity is for George Eliot, author of *Silas Marner* (Macmillan), and you may make copies of it for your class.

IN CLASS

1 Divide the students into groups of about four, and give each group a copy of the cloudscape. Provide the information randomly and encourage your students to begin reading anywhere. It is suggested that at this stage you should allow the groups no more than five minutes to read. Ask the members of the group to tell each other very quickly what they have learnt.

2 Next, ask each group to write four questions which they will ask to students of other groups. These should be of a general comprehension type and designed to check facts only. Ask the students to create questions to suit their own interests.

3 Hold a brief inter-group question and answer session. Tell the students that they can skim and scan the cloudscape to answer any questions to which they cannot remember the answers.

4 When the groups have exhausted their question and answer session, ask them to place the numbers of the relevant clouds under the following headings:

'Childhood & Adolescence', 'Middle Years', 'Later Life'

They do not have to put the numbers of the clouds in order and they must decide for themselves where one period ends and the next begins.

5 When all the groups have completed this stage, ask for feedback. Allow for the fact that adolescence will end at different times for different groups and that later life will also start at different times. The differences can be discussed, but there is no need for uniformity at this stage.

6 Still in groups ask the students to attempt to arrange the numbers they have under each heading in chronological order. Ask them to give you the numbers, so that you can write them on the blackboard in the order they suggest. After discussion a class consensus should be reached and a common order agreed upon. Your role should be that of a scribe and you should not interfere in the decision-making.

7 Now re-divide the class into three groups corresponding to the three headings: 'Childhood', 'Middle Years' and 'Later Life'. The class should then agree about where each group starts and ends.

8 Within each group each student is given responsibility for one or two of the clouds. Each student concerned must expand his or her information, which is only in note form, so that it makes complete sense and flows coherently into the next piece of information. Allow them time to expand the information and to practise with the student who precedes and follows them.

9 Each student then contributes to a chain biography of the author. As an option the biography can be taped with incidental music suggested by the students and with any other effects to which they have access. This also works very well on video with any illustrations (old photographs, maps, letters, etc.) which the students can find.

10 Ask the students to return to their original groups of four. In these groups ask them to select two clouds or events for childhood and adolescence, two for middle years, and two for later life. The criteria for the selection must be that these events are considered by the students in that group to have had the greatest effect on the writer's life and, therefore, on his or her work with its content and ideas.

11 When they have made their selections the students share them with the rest of the class, either via the teacher, or by sending three members of the group to visit the other groups while one of them 'stays at home'.

12 The class can then be asked to compile their Top Ten which shows their responses to the author's life. Number 1 would be the incident which most of the students feel would have a lasting and noticeable effect upon the writer and the particular work. As the class actually reads the book they can alter the positions on their Top Ten.

COMMENT

This activity is time-consuming. However, on a cognitive level, it enables students to practise listening, speaking, reading and writing, and to digest information without consciously memorizing it; while on the affective level, it enables students to identify with the author and his or her life and also encourages them to voice their opinions.

3 1878 George Lewes died. M.A. overcome with grief

19 Father = affectionate/puritanical/forceful

4 1841 Isaac married. Mary Ann and father move → Coventry

6 Met Charles Bray in Coventry. C.B. = philosopher/ Mary Ann stops going to church.

18 Studied languages/ literature/music Greek/Latin/Hebrew/Italian/Spanish

2 Spent childhood/beautiful farmland /Warwickshire

1 1836 mother died Mary Ann took charge

5 Real name = Mary Ann Evans

8 Born 22nd November 1819

20 1849 Father died → travelled widely

15 1851 Assistant Editor of 'Westminster Review.' Non-fiction

17 Stories immediate success. First novel 1859

16 In school holidays happy with company of father and brother

7 1880 died a few months after marriage to John Cross

21 1861 "Silas Marner"

14 G.L. persuades M.A. to write fiction

12 Very close to brother Isaac

10 3 brothers & 1 sister

23 Mother = 2nd wife from a superior family

22 Age 5 → Dame School with Isaac

9 Lived early life on farm in Nuneaton

13 1854 met George Lewes G.L. unhappily married: left wife Mary Ann lives with G.L.

24 Lewes influence → fiction 1856 "Scenes from Clerical Life" by 'George Eliot'

11 Age 6 → Boarding School Influence of principal Miss Lewis

7 Vocabulary

7.1 Word box

LITERARY AIM

Anticipation of lexical problems. Subjective response to meaning. Awareness of power of single items

LEVEL

Elementary to Advanced

TIME

45–60 minutes

INTRODUCTION

The vocabulary in a Reader can sometimes be an obstacle to enjoyment. However, if it is dealt with within the context of a discussion the vocabulary can stimulate students instead of discouraging them.

There are three stages to this activity:

1 Dictionary research
2 Word searching with the puzzle box
3 Discussing the students' responses to the words and categorizing those responses

PREPARATION

Make a word square.

IN CLASS

1 Before the students begin to read you should decide which semantic field the Reader makes the most use of, for example, farming, marriage, ships and shipping terms. Find all the examples of this field in the Reader. The field will probably include words which the student already knows as well as new words. Present the list of words to the students and allow them time to do dictionary research for the words they do not yet know.

2 Make a 'word puzzle' of the words which you would like the students to focus on during the discussion and the reading. The words in the puzzle can read in any direction and they are surrounded by a random selection of letters which should not make any other, unnecessary words. (See the examples at the end of this activity which may be copied for classroom use.)

Divide the students into two teams, or let them work in pairs. Any student who finds a word in the puzzle and can give an explanation of that word can circle it and claim it.

3 When all the words have been found, claimed and explained, ask the students, still in pairs, to categorize the words under certain headings which will evoke a subjective response.

The first example is to do with ships and can be used with *The Poseidon Adventure* (OUP). The second example is to do with marriage and can be used with 'The Courtship of Susan Bell', *Outstanding Short Stories* (Longman).

The words in the shipping field could be categorized under the following headings:

Safety	Danger	Adventure

The words in the marriage field could be categorized as follows:

Old-fashioned	Necessary	Unpleasant

Ask the students to justify their categorizations, and to suggest other categories of their own.

The discussion which this activity generates can lead into the Reader itself. The vocabulary is not so strange when they see it in the new context.

EXAMPLE 1

```
                    L               T               P
                    L               E               O
              F  U  N  N  E  L  S  W  E  R  C
              W  H  E  E  L  E  A  C  Y  T  A
        R  D  R  A  W  E  T  S  N  A  A  H  B  H  H
        A  E  N  G  I  N  E  C  C  P  W  O  I  A  T
  R  E  D  E  G  D  I  R  B  O  H  T  G  L  N  T  R  O  P
     L  I  F  E  B  E  L  T  P  O  A  N  E  K  C  E  D
        O  N  O  O  L  A  S  E  R  I  A  S  O  H  B
           C  O  M  P  A  S  S  E  N  G  E  R  S
```

anchor   crew   hull   saloon
berth   deck   lifebelt   steward
bridge   engine   passengers   telescope
cabin   funnels   port   wheel
captain   gangway   portholes
compass   hatch   radio

EXAMPLE 2

A	B	C	X	T	R	O	T	I	U	S	K	J	M	L
C	A	B	K	J	E	C	N	A	I	F	L	P	Q	O
O	N	W	C	K	J	M	E	P	T	B	J	U	D	V
U	N	V	K	E	L	A	M	A	R	R	I	A	G	E
R	S	B	F	D	F	B	E	K	J	B	M	R	L	N
T	B	I	K	L	B	A	G	M	N	Q	O	K	Y	D
S	W	E	E	T	H	E	A	R	T	O	U	N	V	N
H	A	O	L	K	M	Q	G	B	M	L	O	H	W	A
I	T	S	O	C	M	P	N	K	V	M	Y	O	Z	B
P	O	B	A	I	L	T	E	X	E	G	U	N	T	S
A	R	K	I	D	N	G	B	R	O	D	U	O	W	U
B	I	W	M	C	P	G	E	K	K	A	I	U	L	H
T	N	E	S	N	O	C	L	A	T	N	E	R	A	P
B	G	D	F	G	H	O	L	P	Q	R	U	W	B	Z
X	Q	K	L	P	B	A	H	J	M	K	Q	T	V	X

courtship	groom	wed	fiancé
sweetheart	bride	ring	wife
suitor	wooing	ceremony	husband
engagement	parental	honour	banns
marriage	consent	love	

Section B
While reading

While reading

Introduction

In recent years students have been encouraged to respond more subjectively to Readers. Unfortunately a large number of teachers still consider the Reader to be simply a longer text for comprehension questions or an opportunity to practise reading aloud. Reading is not a passive skill. When we read we search for meaning, drawing upon the complex network of associations which native speakers have at their disposal. Students should be actively engaged in negotiation for meaning. The use of classroom Readers should place emphasis only upon the recycling of facts and key language. Students must be taught how to read and respond to books and not simply to answer questions. During lessons students must be involved in activities which enable them to respond cognitively, emotionally and imaginatively to imaginative writing.

Several of the activities found in section B can be adapted for use in section C (and vice versa).

1 Working with plot

1.1 Whatever next

LITERARY AIM   **Close analysis of plot, based on partial reading of text**

LEVEL   **Intermediate to Advanced**

TIME   **30–40 minutes**

PREPARATION   If the plot of the Reader reaches a rather exciting point, or some sort of a watershed, stop the reading at a suitable point and prepare a list of possible outcomes and hypotheses about what could happen to each of the key characters. Always include the genuine outcome among the possibilities, but do not confirm or reject any of the ideas that the students have.

IN CLASS   Once you have reached the appropriate point in the Reader, divide the students into groups and ask them to consider the several possibilities of what could happen to the key characters, giving reasons for their choice of what is the most likely outcome.

The following example is for use with *Silas Marner* (Macmillan). This story takes a leap forward of sixteen years at one point. Before the students continue reading you should invite them to hypothesize about what could happen to the characters during the sixteen-year interval. They should base their hypotheses on what they have already read along with their ideas of what would make an interesting plot. This does not necessarily coincide with the author's ideas.

Which of these possible futures do you think is most likely for each of the main characters? Why?

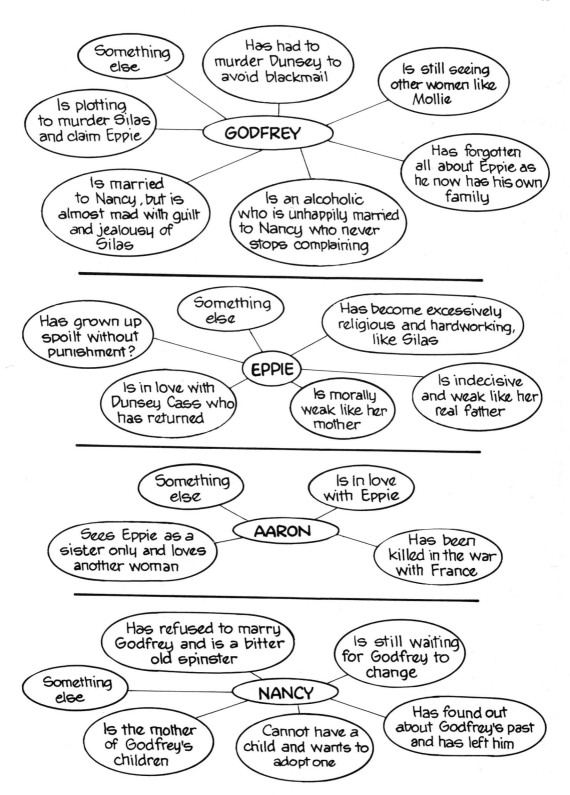

1.2 What was it about?

LITERARY AIM   Interpretation of events, consideration of differing perceptions

LEVEL   Elementary to Advanced

TIME   20–30 minutes

PREPARATION   Prepare three different versions of what the chapter was about. Whilst the versions should be different enough to cause debate they should be similar enough not to distort the facts, and offer instead different interpretations of the same events.

The following examples are for the first section of *Sunnyvista City* (OUP). The students should not have read any further at this stage.

Summary 1

Dan thinks that his wife, Tina, is stupid. She cannot remember anything about where they are. Dan is angry with her because she wants to make pots and soup bowls and sit beside the swimming pool. He wants to go home because he is not enjoying his holiday. Tina gets tired very quickly and does not listen to anything Dan says about the hotel. She is enjoying her holiday very much.

Summary 2

Dan is very ill. He is not eating and not sleeping properly. He wakes up very early every day. He does not take his drugs and when he sleeps in a chair, has bad dreams. Tina wants Dan to feel better. When he is better they can go home and leave the hospital. Tina is trying to help Dan but he does not want to get better.

Summary 3

Dan and Tina are married to each other but they are not happy. They do not like doing the same things. Dan likes to wake up early. Tina likes to sleep. Tina likes pottery, tennis and videos, but Dan does not. Dan wants to go to another hotel. He is not enjoying the holiday. He doesn't like the food. Tina will not listen to him. They are going to fight about the holiday.

IN CLASS   1 Give out copies of the three summaries and ask your students to read them.

2 A discussion should follow as to whether they think any of the versions are accurate. If any of the students decide that none of the summaries is completely accurate, ask them to write their own brief interpretations of events.

3 A discussion of their own summaries can follow.

COMMENT

This technique can be used with equal success at the end of the entire Reader, or at the end of sections or chapters. This activity was first demonstrated to me by Alan Maley.

1.3 Chapter and verse

LITERARY AIM

Selection of key points and impressions; subjective mini-summaries

LEVEL

Elementary to Advanced

TIME

20 minutes

PREPARATION

None.

IN CLASS

1 Ask the students to provide either an alternative chapter heading to the one given in the Reader, or a suggested title for the chapter they have just read, if no heading has been provided. Keep a record of all the suggestions.

2 Ask them to write their own suggestion down the page vertically. They should then write associated ideas horizontally alongside the suggestion, the first letter of each idea being part of the vertical wording. The new title serves as a mini-summary of each chapter.

EXAMPLE 1

Chapter 1 of *Animal Farm* (Longman) was renamed 'Manor Farm' by one group of students, and their mini-summary read as follows:

M an is always the problem
A lways drunk and greedy
N o production
O nly uses us
R ats and rabbits will be friends
F ight against man
A ll animals are equal
R ebellion is necessary
M an must go.

EXAMPLE 2

Chapter 1 of *Scottish Adventure* (Heinemann) was renamed 'Brother' with the following mini-summary:

B itterly cold
R oads are difficult
O n his way by car
T hin carpet of snow
H is sister is waiting
E scape from London
R ests at Newtonmore

1.4 Story map

LITERARY AIM	Selection, ordering and interpreting of key events
LEVEL	Elementary to Advanced
TIME	30–40 minutes on each occasion

INTRODUCTION

A visual record in the form of a map or chart can be fun to do as well as being a method of reinforcing the content of the Reader. Such records should be kept in stages as the book is being read and while interest in the text is high.

PREPARATION

Many stories lend themselves to this diagrammatic treatment. *Around the World in Eighty Days* (OUP), could be attractively summarized on a large map of the world which either you or your students could produce. (See example 1 at the end of this activity.) Coloured ribbons could lead from place to place marking the progress of the characters as they journey around the world. At each place, cards which have the following headings, are stuck on to the map:

– Where?
– Who was there?
– Who did they meet?
– Where did they visit?
– What did they do?
– What was the problem?

IN CLASS

Divide the class into groups or pairs and ask the students to supply and write in the information required by the headings. They should not begin a new section of the Reader until a card for the previous section has been placed in the appropriate location on the map.

VARIATIONS

The *Scottish Adventure* (Heinemann) could be interpreted in a similar way using the map provided at the start of the Reader to chart the events which happen in Aviemore, Scotland. In the *Black Cat* (Heinemann) a map of Egypt, Greece, and Italy can be found at the start of the Reader. The policeman's pursuit of the robbers could be traced on this map. *The Thirty-Nine Steps* (Longman) requires a map of England and Scotland and perhaps a more detailed one of London. *The Poseidon Adventure* (OUP) requires a map of the Aegean and a plan of a ship.

Maps are not much use if the action takes place in one location only. Look at the plot in terms of its time span. If all the action takes place within twenty-four hours, then two clock faces could be used instead of a map and the cards bearing information placed around the clock at the appropriate times. (See example 2.)

If the time span is over several years and involves several characters then the story could be presented as a series of parallel lines extending all the way around the room if necessary. (See example 3.) Each line could represent a character and at various stages along the lines the events which happen can be written on cards and put on to the appropriate time line. This is a very useful technique when looking at plots which do not present events in the order in which they actually happen. The result is a 'Time Frieze' around the room. As suggested before such projects are too weighty to leave until after the book is completed and should be done while the book is being read.

EXAMPLE 1

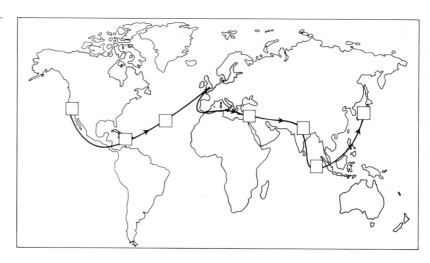

Map showing direction taken with cards providing more information.

EXAMPLE 2

If action takes place in one day use a clockface and cards.

EXAMPLE 3

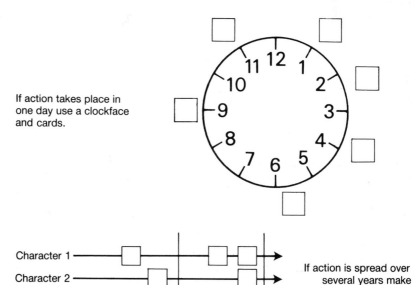

If action is spread over several years make time lines.

1.5 Chain summary

LITERARY AIM	**Summarizing, retelling, interpretation**
LEVEL	**Elementary to Advanced**
TIME	**5–10 minutes per day**
PREPARATION	None.

IN CLASS

If class sets are prohibitively expensive or Readers are in permanent, desperately short supply (i.e., you only have one or two books for the entire class) try to turn this to your advantage and give the Reader to a different student each night. Ask that student to read only one or two pages, and the next day or lesson ask him or her to report orally to the rest of the class what has happened in the story so far, making it as interesting and exciting as possible. Encourage the rest of the class to ask the student more detailed questions.

1.6 Write what wasn't written

LITERARY AIM	**Interpretation and expansion of event**
LEVEL	**Intermediate to Advanced**
TIME	**45–60 minutes**

INTRODUCTION

An author frequently makes an oblique reference to an incident or piece of information. Students can expand upon this so that the information can become, in a way, part of the Reader. The following examples illustrate this.

PREPARATION None.

IN CLASS

1 In 'The Man Who Could Work Miracles', *Outstanding Short Stories* (Longman), the leading protagonist wishes that a policeman could be firstly in hell, and secondly in San Francisco. Ask the students to write a description of the policeman's brief visit to hell, what he saw and what happened to him.

2 At the close of 'The Model Millionaire', *Outstanding Short Stories* (Longman), the philanthropic Baron makes a speech at the wedding of the hero and heroine. Ask the students to write that speech.

3 In *Around the World in Eighty Days* (OUP) the detective, Mr Fix, sends a telegram asking for a warrant to arrest Fogg in Bombay. Ask the students to write that telegram.

4 The missing information can only be attempted after a lengthy class discussion about what this type of document usually contains and what it would contain in this specific instance. The lesson can follow your usual pattern for composition preparation, but in this case the composition is contextualized within the Reader, and you should encourage your students to be as faithful to that context as possible.

5 An entire Reader can be summarized in this way with the students following the progress of the characters and supplying any information which the author did not include.

1.7 Story consequences

LITERARY AIM   **Selecting, ordering, and interpretation of event**

LEVEL   **Elementary to Advanced**

TIME   **30 minutes**

PREPARATION   You should prepare a skeleton of the story-line for the students to complete. This skeleton does not have to be for the entire story; it could be for a section which has just been completed. Also the students could complete the skeleton while they are reading a section.

IN CLASS   **1** Ask the students to fill in the gaps in the story skeleton in the way which seems to them to be most appropriate.

2 The different versions can be discussed with the class. The following example is for 'The Man Who Could Work Miracles', *Outstanding Short Stories* (Longman).

At the start of the story _____ . Fotheringay demonstrates this when _____ . At home he does tricks with _____ . He continues to experiment next morning when _____ . After work he _____ . P.C. Winch tries to stop him, but _____ . Mr Fotheringay visits _____ and reforms _____ . Mr Maydig suggests _____ . As a result _____ . So _____ . The story ends up with _____ .

VARIATION   An alternative approach could be as follows:

Provide the cues as for the previous example. Divide the students into groups of four. This time each student should fold the paper over after having filled one gap. The paper is then passed to the next student who will fill in the second gap and so on, until the story, or section of the story, has been completed as a chain or round by the group. The completed stories can be shared with the whole class. This can be made more demanding for advanced students by working on several stories simultaneously.

2 Working with character

2.1 Wanted

LITERARY AIM	**Interpretation of character, selection and ordering of descriptive detail; representation in visual form of ideas from text**
LEVEL	**Elementary to Advanced**
TIME	**60 minutes minimum**
INTRODUCTION	Designing a 'Wanted' or 'Missing' poster is an entertaining way of asking students to write brief descriptions of any character who is either in trouble with the police, or whose whereabouts are unknown by another character.
PREPARATION	None.

IN CLASS

1 First of all, ask the students for ideas as to what is usually found on these posters. Suggestions usually include the following:
- whether the character is wanted or missing
- the person's name and address
- a photograph or drawing or indentikit picture
- a brief description of appearance
- age
- what they were last seen wearing
- where they were last seen
- who they are usually seen with
- the reason people want this person
- the reward, if any
- who to contact with information

2 Ask the students, either in groups or individually to design a 'Wanted' or 'Missing' poster.

3 A Reader with a crime or a misdemeanour of some sort in it lends itself very easily to this treatment, for example, *The Black Cat* (Heinemann), *The Thirty-Nine Steps* (Longman), and *The Stranger* (Heinemann). However, less obvious stories can suggest posters too, for example, *The Piper of Hamelin* (OUP) produced the poster idea opposite.

WANTED
~The Piper~

for kidnapping our children

Last seen by a young crippled boy. The Piper usually wears a red shirt, blue trousers and a green cape. He plays a pipe. This pipe is dangerous. Usually travels alone. Contact The Lord Mayor of Hamelin with information. Reward of gold coins for information.

2.2 Character graphs

LITERARY AIM Interpretation of character assessment and representation of opinion in graphic, visual form

LEVEL Elementary to Advanced

TIME 50–60 minutes

PREPARATION None.

IN CLASS 1 Divide the class into groups according to the number of key characters in the Reader. For each character decide on a limited number of personality traits you wish the students to note, for example, humour, energy, intelligence, bravery, and loyalty.

2 Ask the students to prepare a graph like the one at the end of this activity (example 1). Ask them to represent each trait with a vertical scale of ten points. The horizontal scale refers to the number of chapters or section into which the Reader is divided.

3 As the students read each chapter the graph can be completed. Under each point in the graph the chapter the students are referring to is described or simply named.

4 When all the graphs have been completed with groups working on different characters, the information can be collated in the form of a bar graph which shows the students findings for all the characters with regard to one trait. (See example 2 at the end of this activity.)

COMMENT The same graph technique can be applied to aspects of the plot and its construction, for example, humour, pathos, suspense, disappointment, boredom, excitement can all be charted chapter by chapter. This is a good way to get students to acknowledge the fact that their emotions do not remain at equilibrium while they are reading, and that an author can attempt to engineer certain responses in a reader.

EXAMPLE 1

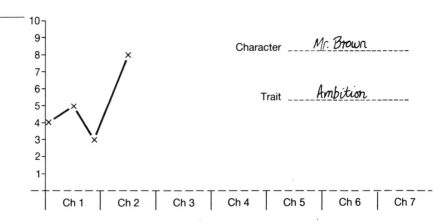

EXAMPLE 2

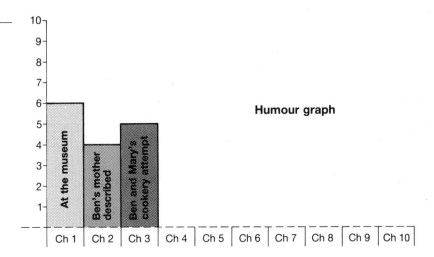

Humour graph

2.3 Give the evidence

LITERARY AIM   Interpretation of specific detail from the text to make general
deductions and assumptions about character

LEVEL   Elementary to Advanced

TIME   30–45 minutes

INTRODUCTION   This activity encourages students to take the specific occurrences or
examples which denote character from the text and apply them
more generally. For example, if someone in the story stops to feed a
stray dog it could be taken in general terms to imply that this
character likes animals and is generous.

PREPARATION   Choose one character from the Reader you are working with. Find
10–15 quotations from the text which could reveal something about
this character's personality.

Then in diagram form provide a list of general statements about the
character's personality which the specific quotations from the text
could be said to illustrate. (See the example at the end of this
activity.)

IN CLASS   1 Ask the students to match up the general quality of the character
with the specific quotation which proves their point. They must be
prepared to explain their choices.
2 Once the students have seen an example of this activity you can
ask them to produce their own matching exercises based on other
characters for other groups to try. It is more interesting at this stage
for it means that the students supply their own interpretations of
the characters' actions and words rather than responding to your
interpretations.

COMMENT   This technique can form the basis for character study work at a
later stage and it encourages the students to base their deductions of
character around the text itself.

The following example comes from 'The Man Who Could Work
Miracles', *Outstanding Short Stories* (Longman).

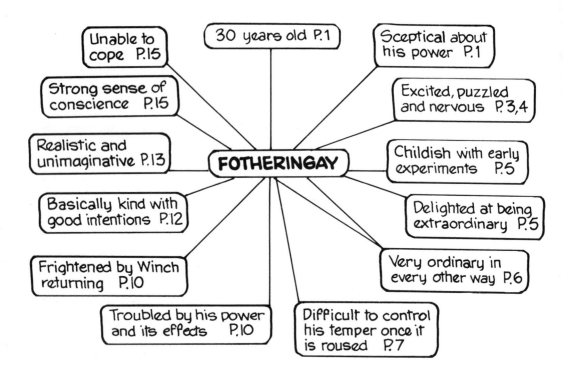

Quotations

a 'Until he was thirty years old . . . .'
b 'Let me be back just before the miracles began.'
c 'There was perhaps a lack of originality in his attempts because apart from his will-power
   Fotheringay was not a very unusual man.'
d 'I don't see how he can understand and he must be angry with me.'
e 'He went home red-faced and hot . . . . watched each street lamp nervously.'
f 'It's three o'clock. I must be going home. I must be at my business by eight o'clock.'
g 'As day passed his state of mind passed from wonder to delight.'
h 'He became violently angry. He turned on the policeman quickly and fiercely.'
i 'He turned a glass of water pink then green.'
j 'He saw that his miracle had gone wrong and a great hatred of miracles came upon him.'
k 'Mr Fotheringay sat with his arm on the table and his head on his arm looking worried.'
l 'Until he was thirty years old Fotheringay did not believe in the power to work miracles.'
m 'These suggestions . . . . it is enough to say they were all kind.'

3 Working with summaries

3.1 Get it wrong

LITERARY AIM	Summarizing, revision of reading. Detailed checking of text for specific information
LEVEL	Elementary to Advanced
TIME	20–30 minutes
INTRODUCTION	Another way to make students look back at one stage of the Reader before progressing to the next is to get them to correct a summary which is full of factual errors as if they were teachers correcting a student's work.
PREPARATION	Prepare a summary (including some deliberate mistakes) of a section of text from the Reader you are working with. (See the example at the end of this activity.)
IN CLASS	The students can work individually or in pairs and they are allowed to look at the Reader. They should cross out the mistake and substitute the correct information. Once students have seen an example they usually enjoy creating their own silly summaries of the next story or section of the Reader for another student to correct.
The following example is for *Silas Marner* (Macmillan).

You are a teacher marking this summary of the chapter. The pupil has made quite a few factual mistakes. Correct the mistakes.

It was a ~~cold~~ [sunny], spring [autumn] ~~Monday~~ [Sunday], ~~seventeen~~ [sixteen] years after Silas had found his new treasure in his cottage. The bells of Raveloe church were ~~broken~~ [ringing] and the villagers were just coming out of church after ~~evening~~ [morning] worship. The humbler people ~~came out before~~ [waited for] the richer ones and one of the ~~first~~ [last] out was ~~Dunsey~~ [Godfrey] Cass, now ~~thirty-five~~ [forty two] years old, a little ~~thinner~~ [fatter] perhaps, but not much different from the Godfrey of twenty-six. Perhaps the ~~elderly~~ [pretty] lady by his side of about ~~fifty~~ [the same age] was more changed, but the high quality of her character showed in her walk and the years had been kind to ~~Priscilla~~ [Nancy].

It was impossible to mistake Silas Marner. His ~~small black~~ [*large brown*] eyes were not so short-sighted now as

is usual with those who have this weakness in youth, but in other ways he seemed very much

~~younger~~ [*older*]. He was ~~sixty~~ [*fifty*]-five, but his bent shoulders and ~~lack of~~ [*white*] hair made him seem much more. ~~In front of him~~ [*By his side*], walked a lovely young girl of ~~eighteen~~ [*sixteen*] with ~~straight black~~ [*curly red-gold*] hair .... They were

welcomed at the cottage by a little brown ~~monkey~~ [*dog*], a pretty little ~~tortoise~~ [*kitten*] and its mother, nor

were these arrivals the only changes in the cottage. The space was filled with good furniture

which had come with the beds from the ~~Rainbow Inn~~ [*Red House*].

3.2 Ordering puzzle

LITERARY AIM

Ordering, revision, remembering what has been read, summarizing

LEVEL

Elementary to Intermediate

TIME

20–30 minutes

INTRODUCTION

If a Reader consists of short stories or chapters in which a confusing amount of action takes place it is often helpful for the students to look back at the chapter or story and get the order of events clear in their minds before proceeding to the next section. This activity resembles a puzzle or game and is, therefore, more attractive to the student as a method of revision. Once students have seen an example of this activity produced by the teacher they are quite enthusiastic about producing their own puzzles at another stage.

PREPARATION

Produce a summary of the story written in short concise sentences. There should not be any more than twenty of these sentences, all of which are set down in the wrong order. (See the example at the end of this activity, which may be copied for classroom use.)

IN CLASS

1 Give out copies of your prepared summary and ask the students to put numbers next to the sentences in the order in which they refer to the story. They may look at the Reader while they do this.

2 Check that everyone has the correct order before proceeding.

3 Supply everyone with a list of cohesive devices suitable for their level. Divide the students into small groups and ask them to try and link as many of these short sentences as possible and make them flow, one into the other. They may change punctuation if they wish.

4 Whilst in their groups ask the students to start telling the story to each other in a round. (They may use the ordering puzzle to help them.) Each student should take one sentence as a stimulus, but any extra information or details they can remember are added in. The most successful group will still be telling the story when all the other groups have dried up. During this stage they are not allowed to look at the Reader.

The following example is for 'The Doll's House', *Outstanding Short Stories* (Longman).

Below you will find a catalogue of the events of the story. Each event roughly corresponds to a paragraph in the story. Write a number 1 in the empty box of the first paragraph and a 2 in that of the second paragraph and so on.

Letter	Event	Event Order
a	Kezia asks her mother if the Kelveys can visit.	
b	The furnishing and fittings are described.	
c	Lena tells the Kelveys that their father is in prison.	
d	Isabel is very popular with the other girls.	
e	The Kelveys are sent away quickly.	
f	Mrs Hay donates a doll's house to the children.	
g	Kezia sees the Kelveys approaching their home.	
h	The school is described.	
i	The other girls tell stories about the Kelveys.	
j	Kezia talks to the Kelveys about the doll's house.	
k	The house is delivered and the children open it.	
l	Kezia and Isabel tell the others about the lamp.	
m	Aunt Beryl interrupts Kezia and the Kelveys.	
n	The Kelveys are described.	
o	The Kelveys take comfort from each other.	
p	The girls anxiously go to school to tell their friends.	
q	Else wants to see the doll's house.	

NOTE: You may make photocopies of this for classroom use (but please note that copyright law does not normally permit multiple copying of published material).

3.3 Acrostic comprehension

LITERARY AIM   Checking of comprehension of facts and ideas, revision,
summarizing

LEVEL   Elementary to Advanced

TIME   20–30 minutes

INTRODUCTION   As well as being a method of handling vocabulary this puzzle
format is an enjoyable way of tackling comprehension, and much
more fun than standard comprehension questions. Like most
question/answer activities it is far more effective if the students
create their own puzzles and try them with each other.

PREPARATION   To prepare these puzzles one must work backwards from the target
answer which can be a name, word, or phrase from the story or
message to the student. The letters which this target comprises will
begin your answers, which ideally should consist of only one word.
The questions and answers should be related to the content of the
Reader.

In the following example the questions refer to 'X-ing a Paragraph',
Outstanding Short Stories (Longman).

1 Bullet-head wrote one which was very severe.	[A] rticle
2 Bullet-head burns this at night.	[L] amp oil
3 Bullet-head is one by profession.	[E] ditor
4 The technique of using X for another letter.	[X] -ing
5 Bob thinks that drinking makes Bullet-head this.	[A] ngry
6 The short name for the town.	[N] opolis
7 The people think the signs are a message to this.	[D] evil
8 With its effect the article is compared with this.	[E] xplosion
9 The chief says nobody will do this.	[R] ead

The answers to the puzzle need not begin with the required letter;
they simply have to include the required letter. Once again there is
a vertical message, but the number of letters either side of this is
precisely indicated with dashes.

```
1         _/_/_____
2       ___/_/____
3       ___/_/_____
4      ____/_/_____
5         _/_/_____
6        __/_/_____
7     _____/_/_____
```

IN CLASS

1 Divide the students into pairs and supply each pair with a copy of your prepared puzzle.

2 After the students have completed the puzzle ask them, in twos, to produce their own puzzle about the next chapter or section of the Reader.

4 Working on interpretation

4.1 Scoop

LITERARY AIM

Interpretation of events through the perspective of 'other than student'. Writing accounts in role

LEVEL

Elementary to Advanced

TIME

60–90 minutes

INTRODUCTION

This activity can be done in the frame of journalists who work for a sensation-seeking newspaper, but this is not absolutely necessary. It is an extension of the newspaper headline pre-reading activity 2.1 exemplified earlier with *The Thirty-Nine Steps* (Longman).

PREPARATION

As with the earlier example the key incidents, either of the chapter, or the entire Reader are set out as headlines on a front page. These headlines should be prepared by you, as before. The difference is that this time the students have already read the chapter or Reader referred to. (See the example at the end of this activity.)

IN CLASS

1 Before allocating responsibilities for individual stories, ask the students to suggest which incidents in the Reader are being referred to by which headline, and which characters from the Reader are being interviewed. Remind them too that journalists have a way of building big stories out of very little information.

2 Ask the students to suggest generally what they would expect to read in each news item about the episodes referred to, and also to suggest what the feelings and impressions would be of the journalist who was either interviewing or writing an eyewitness account. For example, would the journalist feel pleased, shocked or afraid?

3 A second copy of the front page should be made. From this copy each individual story shape should be cut out. If there are six stories divide the class into six groups. In each group appoint a sub-editor who has responsibility for checking grammar and spelling.

4 Give each group a list of the relevant sections or pages of the Reader where they are to go 'on location' to get more information for their story. Encourage them to extend the facts imaginatively by reading between the lines, in order to come up with an exciting story. They cannot alter anything which happened in the Reader, but they can extend and enhance it.

5 Alternatively, give some students roles as characters from the Reader and allow them to be interviewed about what happened to them. After the interview they can assist the sub-editor in checking the story and making sure that they are not misrepresented in the news story.

6 Each sub-editor, when happy with the story, gives it to the Editor (teacher) who does any final checking. The stories are then glued into position on the second copy of the front page. Any gaps can be filled with pictures which the students feel are suitable to accompany their stories.

7 The final front page with all six stories can be displayed or photocopies can be made for the students to have. The activity encourages re-reading, summarizing, imaginative writing, pride in presentation and genuine communication within each group as the story gets written. The Editor can, if she or he wishes, add the extra touch of authenticity by introducing a deadline by which all copy must be ready for printing. This can help certain groups to pace themselves.

The following example is for *Animal Farm* (Longman), chapter two, and shows how one class of students responded to the newspaper stimulus.

Willingdon Gazette

Shocked Farmer tells of Animal Rebellion

We met Mr Jones at the Red Lion after the rebellion. He was so shocked that he spoke to us with much difficulty. He had left his farm on Midsummer's Eve and gone to Willingdon for a drink. He stayed until the next day. "But my men had to be there all that time," he said angrily. "They had to take care of the animals. It's not my fault all this situation. When I'm absent my men prefer to enjoy themselves.

That's why I'm out of my farm", he continued. And he told us his men had forgotten to feed the animals for two days. The animals got so hungry they broke down the door of the store shed. At that time "I had to protect my farm," he told us. But the animals became angry and started to butt and kick. "It was a terrible sight and it all happened so suddenly," said Jones.

Witnesses tell of Bonfire Celebration

I stood behind a tree, outside the farm land, and what I saw was frightening and surprising! After Mr and Mrs Jones and their men had gone, all the animals, sure no one was hiding in the yard, lit a big fire. Then they collected every instrument that Mr Jones used to make them feel pain, such as bits, nose rings, dog chains, halters and whips and threw them on the fire. A pig, I suppose it was one of their leaders, threw on the fire some ribbons and an enormous, proud horse also threw a hat.

Then another large pig led all the animals into the store shed and gave them something to eat.

In a little while they all came out again; they seemed happy. And finally, in great enthusiasm, they all sang a song, not only once but five times.

You won't believe it, but I found myself singing this song and crying! It was a real celebration.

NEW LEADER MAKES LAWS

I decided to go to the farm building. There I saw Snowball and Napoleon send for a ladder which they put against the end wall of the barn.

They made laws by which all the animals on Animal Farm must live for ever. They gave the laws the name of 7 Commandments. The commandments were written on the tarred wall in great white letters that I could read thirty yards away. They were:

1. Whatever goes on two legs is an enemy.
2. Whatever goes on four legs or has wings is a friend.
3. No animal shall wear clothes.
4. No animal shall drink alcohol.

5. No animal shall sleep in a bed.
6. No animal shall kill another animal.
7. All animals are equal.

All the animals nodded and tried to learn the commandments. We are watching and waiting for their results.

Farmer's Wife Flees

After the unbelievable rebellion of the animals at Mr Jones' farm last night, which surprised and shocked every human being in England, Mrs Jones was interviewed by our newspaper. We asked Mrs Jones to describe the unfortunate night that changed life on Manor Farm. Unfortunately, Mrs Jones could not easily answer as she was in a terrible condition. She repeated several times that the rebellion was unexpected. She believed it was only a nightmare and she would wake up in her bed. Unfortunately, last night was reality. Her wish will not come true.

ANIMALS TOUR FARM- HOUSE

It was unbelievable! I saw the whole thing as I was hidden behind some bushes close to the farm buildings. The animals halted outside the building. They looked frightened to go inside. Snowball and Napoleon found the solution by butting the door open. The animals entered. Then they tiptoed from room to room. They gazed at the unbelievable luxury, at the feather mattresses, horse hair sofa. When they found some hams in the kitchen they buried them. The purpose of the animals is still unknown.

4.2 Playmaking

LITERARY AIM

Interpretation of character and event through the perspective of 'other than student'. Discussion and interpretation in role

LEVEL

Intermediate to Advanced

TIME

60 minutes minimum

INTRODUCTION

This activity has double value in that it enables students to communicate freely and imaginatively about the Reader, while at the same time they also use the author's words for the dramatic parts, thereby removing the fear that some students have about improvising. This technique is extremely useful for Readers which have long stretches of dialogue in them.

PREPARATION

Before the lesson take the section of the Reader you wish to dramatize and extract all the dialogue from it. Rewrite the dialogue as a dramatic script with the characters' names in the margin alongside their spoken words. Leave spaces before and within the dialogue for stage directions. The students will be supplying their own stage directions. See the example given at the end of this activity.

WARM-UP

1 First of all, introduce the idea of stage directions and demonstrate through a simple example how a change in the direction can alter our interpretation of what is going on:

'Oh! It's you!' (with surprise)
'Oh! It's you!' (with fear, moving back)
'Oh! It's you!' (with relief, moving forwards)

2 Ask the students to practise these little exchanges with each other following the stage directions. Then they can write some stage directions of their own for this little speech. Encourage them to be imaginative. Tell each student that they are the director and that they must coach another student to say this brief speech according to their direction. The results of this can be shared with the rest of the class in a very light-hearted way.

IN CLASS

1 Divide the class into groups according to how many characters are involved. Any spare students can be allocated to groups as directors.

2 Ask the students to look at the Reader in a new light as they try to solve the problems of how the characters spoke, moved and reacted to each other's words. At any time during the lesson, if space permits, encourage the groups to get up and try out what they have decided.

3 If the groups feel confident enough they can share their interpretations of the scene with the other students. This is not essential and students should not be forced to do this. The object of the lesson is not to perform but to discuss and evaluate the Reader from another perspective.

The following example is from *Silas Marner* (Macmillan). No additional dialogue has been supplied. The students are free to interpret the scene as they wish. Interpretations usually range from melodrama to pantomime with serious attempts at pathos in between. The author's words come to life for the students whichever interpretation they choose.

An excerpt from 'The Lost Treasure'
A play in one act from *Silas Marner*

Silas [   ] At first I used to feel that you might be changed into the gold again, but that didn't last long. I began to feel the need of your looks and your voice and the touch of your little fingers. I wouldn't have wanted the gold if it had taken you from me. You didn't know when you were little, Eppie, how old father Silas loved you.

Eppie [   ] But I know now, Father, and if it hadn't been for you there'd have been no one to love me.

Silas [   ] Ah, my child, the blessing was mine! If you hadn't been sent to save me I should have died in my misery. You see how the money was kept until it was wanted for you. Our life is very wonderful. The money means nothing to me now. I don't think it ever would again unless I lost you, Eppie.

[   ] Enter GODFREY and NANCY

Nancy [   ] We're disturbing you very late, my dear.

Godfrey [   ] Well, Marner, it's a great comfort to me to see you with your money again. It's a great sorrow to me that it was one of my family that did you the wrong, and I feel I ought to make up to you for it in every way. Whatever I can do for you will be nothing but paying a debt, in other matters as well as the robbery.

Silas [   ] Sir, I've much to thank you for already. The robbery wasn't your fault.

Godfrey [   ] You may look at it that way, Marner, but I never can, and I hope you will let me do what I think right. You're getting rather old for such close work as weaving, Marner. It's time you stopped and had some rest. You look tired, though you're not an old man, are you?

Silas [   ] Fifty-five as far as I know, sir.

Godfrey [   ] Well, you may have thirty years longer yet and that money on the table, after all, is only a little. It won't go far if you've nobody to keep but yourself and you've had two to keep for many years now.

Silas [   ] I'm in no fear of want, sir. Eppie and I will manage very well. Very few working people have as much money saved as that. It may not seem much to you, but it's almost too much for us. We don't want much.

Eppie [   ] Only the garden, Father.

4.3 Dear diary

LITERARY AIM

Interpretation of character and event through subjective reading and writing

LEVEL

Intermediate to Advanced

TIME

25 minutes on each occasion

INTRODUCTION

Introduce this activity with a brief exchange of ideas about what is usually kept in diaries, and the differences between a personal diary and a business one. Students usually suggest the following ideas for inclusion in a diary:

events that have happened that day
things that were said
reminders
hopes and fears
disappointments and plans
secret thoughts

After students suggest ideas about what could be included in a diary, they can then direct their attentions to the Reader. They can keep diaries of the events as seen by more than one character, thus helping them to keep a record of events, and to identify with the characters. If the story spans several days and involves several characters the events of those days would be seen differently by each of the students according to the information they had and the experiences they had shared.

IN CLASS

1 Explain to the class that *Around the World in Eighty Days* (OUP) is a Reader which lends itself well to this treatment as each of the protagonists has differing amounts of information at varying times, and there are several independent experiences as well as shared ones.

2 Divide the class into three groups – one for Phileas Fogg, one for Passepartout his servant, and one for Mr Fix the detective who is pursuing them – then three different diaries could be kept charting their progress around the world. As the story continues the diary style usually becomes more sympathetic.

3 If the story takes place over a short period of time then only two or three diary entries are required: one which shows what life was like on the average day before the adventure starts; the entry for the day on which it starts; and the entry for the day when the story ends. These entries should show the effect the action has had upon the characters involved.

4 If the story of the Reader spans several years then only the key events need be recorded. For example, the story of *Silas Marner* (Macmillan) spans thirty-two years, but it can be recorded in eight to ten diary entries. In this case the relationships developing between the characters would be of interest as well as a record of events.

COMMENT

This approach can also be used with Readers such as *Scottish Adventure* (Heinemann), *The Piper of Hamelin* (OUP) and *Hijacked* (OUP), all of which have plots which span a very limited time.

4.4 Pyramid discussion

LITERARY AIM

Consideration of varying views held on theme. Discussion of those views subjectively

LEVEL

Intermediate to Advanced

TIME

50–60 minutes

INTRODUCTION

This activity is so called because the number of students involved in the discussion grows in the same way a pyramid grows, for example:

1
22
4444

PREPARATION

First prepare a list of statements, clichés and opinions about the subject for discussion – in this case the theme of a Reader. This list should be as varied in viewpoint as possible and not reflect your own opinion only. (See the example given at the end of this activity.)

IN CLASS

1 Ask the students to read the statements individually, and in silence, and decide on which ones they agree with.

2 Ask them to rank the statements in order, according to how much they agree, or to reduce the list from ten points to only five.

3 Then put the students into pairs where they must repeat the task, and after discussion, come up with an order or selection based upon compromise. When agreement has been reached, put the students into fours and ask them to repeat the activity. Finally, groups of eight can decide upon the order or selection they want.

COMMENT

The advantage of this activity is that students repeat their arguments several times as the pyramid grows.

The following example is one suitable for use with the Reader *Hijacked* (OUP).

Arrange these statements in order according to how strongly you agree with them. Number 1 will go next to the statement which you agree with most strongly and number 10 will go next to the statement which you agree with least.

1 The only hero in a hijack is a dead hero.

2 Governments should never give in to the demands of terrorists.

3 It is the airline's responsibility to make sure that passengers are safe.

4 Terrorists have no choice. Society will only listen to minority groups after extreme and violent action.

5 The crew of the plane should be armed and always try to fight off the terrorists.

6 The police should give the terrorists what they want and get the passengers freed. Then they can break promises.

7 Terrorism is just a fact of life now and all travellers should be prepared for it.

8 Passengers should be sacrificed. People are less important than principles.

9 The passengers should try to overpower the terrorists.

10 It is because of bad security in airports that terrorism is increasing.

5 Working on listening

5.1 Listen and write

LITERARY AIM	Focusing attention on specific details to highlight them through listening activities; revise what has been read
LEVEL	Elementary to Advanced
TIME	20–30 minutes

INTRODUCTION It is possible to give students extra listening practice by using the Reader as a source of material. Exercises involving matching, multiple choice items, true-false questions and information transfer can all be designed by you to accompany extracts from the simplest Reader. However, it is more rewarding for all involved to have older or more experienced students design the activities for younger ones. Advanced students can design for intermediate students, and intermediate students for elementary students.

PREPARATION Either you or your more proficient/older students prepare the listening material. The reading passage does not have to be read 'live' by you. Instead, you can tape the reading, or older students can be readers for younger, less proficient classes.

IN CLASS 1 Give each student a copy of the listening exercises. Remind them, or ask them to remind you, of what has been read already.

2 Allow the students some time to look at the questions. Then read the extract to them once. During this first listening they should not try to answer the questions.

3 Read the piece a second time. During the second reading the students should try to answer the questions.

The following exercises were used with *Rip Van Winkle* (Longman).

As Rip came nearer he was surprised at what he saw. He saw a short, square, old man with long hair and a long beard. His hair was nearly white, but his clothes were like the clothes that Dutchmen wore in the year 1600. The old man was carrying a small barrel on his back. Rip took it and carried it for him. They climbed up a narrow place. As they went up, Rip heard a deep sound—a long, rolling sound like the sound of big guns, or like thunder. (But there was no rain and there were no thunder clouds.)

As they went on, Rip saw two big rocks in front; the sound seemed to come from the other side of them.

'Why,' Rip wondered, 'why is he carrying that little barrel up the mountain? Why? Where is he going?' But Rip was afraid to ask. They went between the rocks and came to a small open space. It was shut in by high rocks on all sides, and trees grew down over it, hiding the sky.

There were some strange looking people in this place. They were dressed like the old man whom Rip had met—like Dutchmen in the year 1600.

Their faces were strange: one man had a very big head and small eyes; another had a very big nose so that his face seemed to be all nose! They all had beards. There was one man who seemed to be their captain. He was fat and round. He had a fine long coat, a high hat with a feather, and his shoes were high at the back with a rose on the front.

They were playing a game of ninepins. None of them spoke, but they rolled the balls at the ninepins, and the noise of the balls made a sound like thunder among the high hills.

1 Which drawing is most like the description of the *captain*?

2 Which year is mentioned? [_ _ _ _ _ _ _ _]

3 Tick the box if the item in the drawing is mentioned in the story.

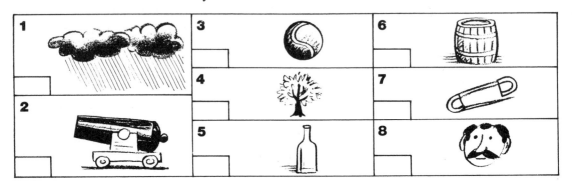

Section C
After reading

After reading

Introduction

Students can acquire confidence and flair with language if allowed to explain where their opinions originated. Leland Roloff in his book *The Perception and Evocation of Literature* (Harvard Press 1973) did not have the class Reader in mind, but the recommendations he makes about teaching literature are highly appropriate:

'The language of literature . . . should enable a student to enter inner worlds which become real to the perceiver.'

Students should be able to enter the 'inner worlds' without the traditional teaching method of comprehension checks. Instead they could be more actively engaged in negotiation for potential meaning, both individually and with other students. Interest in the activity can sustain interest in the text or be fuelled by interest in the text.

The activities in this section are generated by the text and extend its potential for meaningful language work. The tasks cannot be performed without the text, that is, they cannot replace the text. Frequently, they involve the students in detailed revision and scrutiny of the author's words, but at all times there is a valid reason for the student to do so, and the various skills being practised and developed in each activity will increase understanding and subsequently pleasure in future Readers.

1 Looking back at character

1.1 Matching

LITERARY AIM

Revise and emphasize associations between characters, speeches, events, locations, etc

LEVEL

Elementary to Advanced

TIME

10–15 minutes

INTRODUCTION

If the Reader has rather a large number of characters and the students are becoming confused about who did what, try a simple matching exercise to help them.

PREPARATION

None.

IN CLASS

1 Write the names of the characters down one side of the blackboard. On the opposite side write a brief description of the characters, but avoid putting the correct description and character together.

2 Ask the students to match characters' names with their corresponding descriptions.

The following example is taken from 'The Man Who Could Work Miracles', *Outstanding Short Stories* (Longman).

A Mr Fotheringay	1 The fat lady who serves drinks
B Toddy Beamish	2 The policeman sent to San Francisco
C Mr Cox	3 One who always disagrees with Fotheringay
D Miss Maybridge	4 The housekeeper who reforms
E A cyclist	5 The clergyman who wants to stop time
F Mr Winch	6 The landlord of the Long Dragon
G Mr Maydig	7 The man with the power to work miracles
H Mrs Minchen	8 One who witnessed the first miracle

1.2 Pelmanism

LITERARY AIM

Revise and emphasize associations between characters, speeches, events, locations, etc

LEVEL

Elementary to Advanced

TIME

30 minutes

PREPARATION

Use the same information as in the previous example and write the characters' names and descriptions on sixteen pieces of card. A set of cards will be required for every pair of students, or for every group of four.

IN CLASS 1 Place the cards face down in four rows of four and in random order.

2 Ask the students to work in pairs or groups of four and take turns at turning two pieces of card face up. If the name and the role correspond they can keep the pair. If the cards do not correspond then they are returned to their positions face down and another student may choose.

3 Students can produce such games very easily once they have seen an example produced by you.

1.3 Character bingo

LITERARY AIM Revision of associations between characters, traits, events, etc

LEVEL Intermediate to Advanced

TIME 30 minutes

PREPARATION None.

IN CLASS 1 Ask students to make their own bingo cards with the names of four characters of their choice on them. For example:

Mrs Minchin	Mr Maydig
Fotheringay	Mr Cox

2 They should also prepare small pieces of paper on which they should write one piece of information about each of the characters on their card and his or her role in the story. They do not mention the character by name.

3 Place the pieces of paper in a bag and draw out at random and read aloud. If a student hears a piece of information which refers to one of the characters on the card she or he crosses off the name. When all four characters on the card have been mentioned the student shouts 'Bingo' and repeats the information she or he heard about her or his character in order to win the game.

1.4 Who am I?

LITERARY AIM Controlled detailed description and exposition of character

LEVEL Elementary to Advanced

TIME 30 minutes

PREPARATION None.

IN CLASS

1 Divide the class into two teams. Ask a student from one of the teams to volunteer to 'be' one of the characters in the Reader. The student supplies information in ten very small amounts about the character.

2 The students in the other team have only one guess and must guess the identity of the character before the student gets to the tenth piece of information. If they guess correctly after only four pieces of information they get six points. (10 minus 4)

3 This activity encourages students to remember small details of characterization.

1.5 Name dropping

LITERARY AIM

Revision of character, selection and interpretation of detail

LEVEL

Elementary to Advanced

TIME

20–30 minutes

PREPARATION

None.

IN CLASS

Instruct the students to compile mini character studies simply by writing a character's name vertically and asking them to supply suitable descriptive terms for that character which begin with those letters. This is illustrated by the following examples:

EXAMPLE 1

A ngry, assertive
N ot nice
G ood gardener
U nhelpful
S ilent, sombre

EXAMPLE 2

```
       ag G ressive
  mother L y
      br A ve
 frightene D
        Y oung
   nervou S
```

1.6 Character posters

LITERARY AIM

Creative response to and revision of character through text and visuals

LEVEL

Elementary to Advanced

TIME

50 minutes minimum

PREPARATION   None.

IN CLASS   1 If the Reader is a selection of short stories, or is particularly full of interesting characters, give the students, in groups, the responsibility of one character only and ask them to represent that character in poster format. You may be required to show an example before the students grasp the idea.

2 Each group should put a representation of the character at the centre of the poster: this can be a drawing or picture from a magazine or a copy of the illustration in the Reader. Around this picture the group assembles all the things said about the character, or said by the character, or their deductions about the character, or a combination of all three ingredients. In fact the students are actually writing character studies, but presenting them as posters.

The following examples of posters arose from the collection *Outstanding Short Stories* (Longman): the first being the teacher's example which was used as a starting point; the other being a sample of students' work.

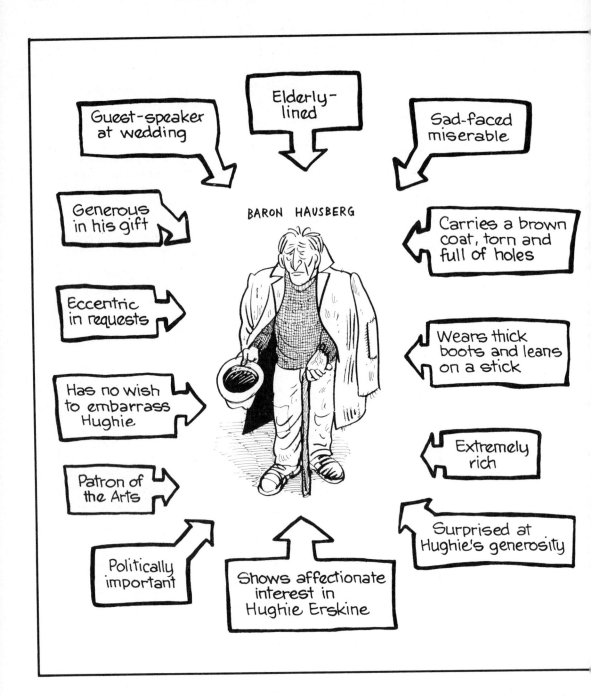

1.7 Character clusters

LITERARY AIM	Recognition of themes and connecting ideas
LEVEL	Elementary to Advanced
TIME	10–15 minutes

PREPARATION

This activity is particularly useful for collections of short stories. Before the lesson you should think of category headings which would include characters from more than one story.

IN CLASS

Ask the students to try classifying characters in cluster groups as a means of encouraging them to gauge similarity and dissimilarity. Give the entire class one central idea such as 'Families'. Ask them to cluster around the central idea all the examples of it which can be found in the collection of stories. When the students have seen one example ask them to make a cluster of their own around a central idea which they have chosen.

The following examples are drawn from the collection *Outstanding Short Stories* (Longman).

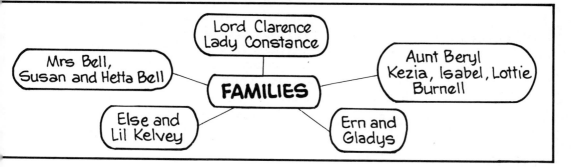

VARIATIONS

Try other key words such as *children, poor, rich, elderly, strong, weak, admirable, attractive* and *pathetic*.

Ask the students to think of as many ways of their own to group the characters according to *appearance, disposition, attributes, possible outcomes, situation* and *role in the plot*.

1.8 Card games

LITERARY AIM

Revision of character, selections of key facts, awareness of what is known

LEVEL

Elementary to Advanced

TIME

30–40 minutes

PREPARATION

Provide each group of four students with a pack of cards. These cards are either prepared by you or by the students themselves in a previous lesson. Each pack comprises two equal sets of cards. The first set has the names of the characters in the Reader. The second set has either a quotation to match one of the names, or an illustration, or a fact about the character. Each character's name has only one other corresponding card. The two sets of cards are combined and shuffled, and then either snap or pelmanism can be played.

IN CLASS

Snap

Deal the players equal numbers of cards without showing them. Then, each player in turn should lay a card face up in a pile in the centre of the table. If two cards relating to the same character are laid consecutively the entire central pile of cards goes to the player who spotted the connection and laid his hand on the pile first. This method is slightly less noisy than shouting 'Snap!' The student who has all the cards at the end of the game is the winner. This game is a very useful revision aid as it requires the student to read, remember and react very quickly.

Pelmanism

Lay all the cards face down in parallel rows. Each student may turn over two cards at a time. If the two cards correspond in some way, for example, a character's name and a quotation from that character, the student can keep both cards. If the cards do not correspond they are turned face down again and returned to exactly the same places, and then the next student takes a turn. The winner is the student who has the most pairs of cards.

The following examples are from *Animal Farm* (Longman).

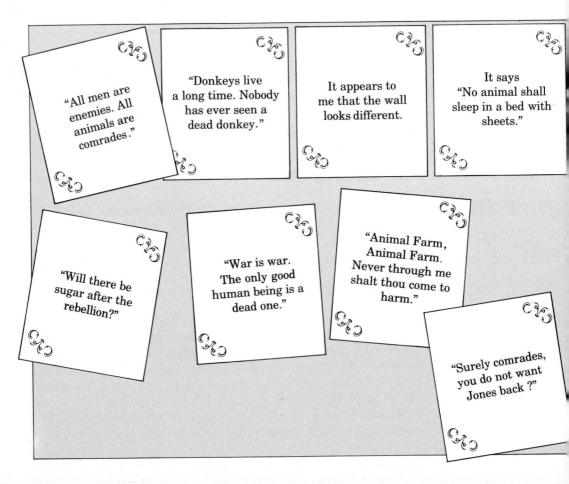

"All men are enemies. All animals are comrades."

"Donkeys live a long time. Nobody has ever seen a dead donkey."

It appears to me that the wall looks different.

It says "No animal shall sleep in a bed with sheets."

"Will there be sugar after the rebellion?"

"War is war. The only good human being is a dead one."

"Animal Farm, Animal Farm. Never through me shalt thou come to harm."

"Surely comrades, you do not want Jones back?"

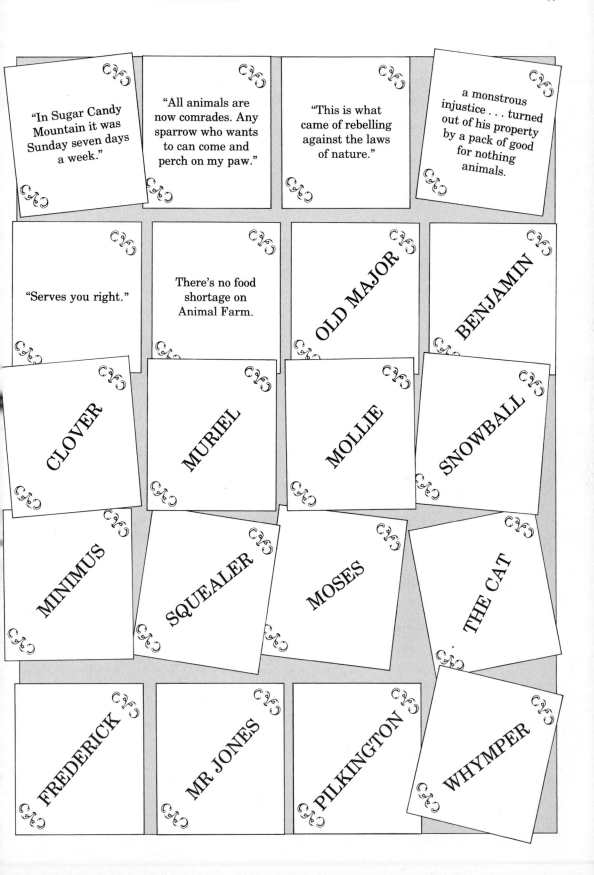

"In Sugar Candy Mountain it was Sunday seven days a week."

"All animals are now comrades. Any sparrow who wants to can come and perch on my paw."

"This is what came of rebelling against the laws of nature."

a monstrous injustice . . . turned out of his property by a pack of good for nothing animals.

"Serves you right."

There's no food shortage on Animal Farm.

OLD MAJOR

BENJAMIN

CLOVER

MURIEL

MOLLIE

SNOWBALL

MINIMUS

SQUEALER

MOSES

THE CAT

FREDERICK

MR JONES

PILKINGTON

WHYMPER

2 Interpreting character

2.1 Grid reference

LITERARY AIM

Revision of character and characteristics through theme

LEVEL

Elementary to Advanced

TIME

20–30 minutes

PREPARATION

You must prepare a grid for every student, or a sample blank grid for every student to copy, or if you are using *Animal Farm* (Longman) or 'The Courtship of Susan Bell', *Outstanding Short Stories* (Longman), you may take photocopies of the grids at the end of this activity.

IN CLASS

1 One very simple way of generating discussion and reflection about character is to use a grid. This grid should have the names of the main protagonists written along the top of it and characteristics, or qualities, or traits written down the side of it. The students should read down the column for each character and where they think that a character has exhibited this trait they should place a cross. The students discuss their responses to the grid and try to justify the presence of a cross.

2 An alternative is to put a number out of ten in the box. Ten means that the character demonstrated this trait to a high degree. This generates far more discussion.

3 By using the grid several layers of information can be supplied at a time. They can be especially useful when reviewing or reflecting upon the various attitudes displayed by a selection of characters to the same problem or person.

COMMENT

The grids given as examples show firstly, certain qualities, etc. of a variety of characters from *Animal Farm*, and secondly, the attitudes to one of the other characters, and to the subject of marriage from 'The Courtship of Susan Bell'. When students have seen samples of these grids they can construct their own in groups.

Animal Farm

Here are the main protagonists in the book. Down the page is a list of qualities. Put a tick in the box if you feel the character possesses the quality to any degree.

ATTRIBUTE, QUALITY, OR CHARACTERISTIC	THE DOGS	MURIEL	OLD MAJOR	SHEEP	PILKINGTON	FREDERICK	WHYMPER	MR JONES	SQUEALER	MOSES	MOLLIE	BENJAMIN	CLOVER	BOXER	SNOWBALL	NAPOLEON
STRONG																
WEAK																
POOR																
RICH																
POLITE																
RUDE																
PATIENT																
GENEROUS																
EMOTIONAL																
BORING																
ATTRACTIVE																
QUIET																
FOOLISH																
WISE																
SINCERE																
FALSE																
ARROGANT																
TALENTED																
HUMBLE																
AGGRESSIVE																
TIMID																
INTELLIGENT																
ARTICULATE																
TACITURN																
TRUSTWORTHY																
EFFICIENT																
ENERGETIC																
LAZY																
CYNICAL																
NAIVE																

	Worried in case she's hurt.	Interfering in her business	Concerned for her future	In love with her
MRS BELL				
HETTA				
AARON				
PHINEAS				

Attitude to Susan

Theme of Marriage

The characters have different ideas about courtship and marriage, although they have points in common.

	Courtship must be slow and steady.	The woman must not speak first.	The parents' consent must be granted.	Young men often amuse themselves with girls.	A steady job is more important than love.	Young people shouldn't be parted.	Marriage is a happy thing and good for people.	Husbands must not be chased.	Young people should not be left alone together.	Promise nothing and do not use first names until sure.	Accept no gifts from gentlemen.
SUSAN											
AARON											
PHINEAS											
HETTA											
MRS BELL											

NOTE: You may make photocopies of this for classroom use (but please note that copyright law does not normally permit multiple copying of published material).

2.2 Balloon debates

LITERARY AIM   Revision, reassessment and discussion of character

LEVEL   Intermediate to Advanced

TIME   30 minutes

PREPARATION   None.

IN CLASS

1 Ask the students to imagine that all the characters from their Reader have been placed in the basket of a hot air balloon. Unfortunately, the balloon has a small hole in it and air is slowly escaping, causing the balloon to fall. One character must be ejected to keep the balloon aloft. Who would the students discard first? Which character should be the last one left in the basket?

2 The criteria the students employ for ejection can be purely subjective, that is, how popular the particular character was as far as they were concerned. However, their criteria could also be based on how essential to the plot or to the theme each character is. What would the story lose if that character were written out?

3 The activity could be improved upon by giving groups special responsibility for ensuring the survival of one particular character and encouraging them to present arguments in favour of the survival of that character against the survival of the others.

2.3 Zodiac

LITERARY AIM   Revision, reassessment and reinterpretation of character and plot through altered perspective

LEVEL   Intermediate to Advanced

TIME   40–50 minutes

PREPARATION   It is fairly easy to find out the basic traits for the signs of the zodiac. Women's magazines as well as a variety of EFL course books provide a breakdown of chief characteristics. If no further information is available the table on the next page can be used, and you may make photocopies for classroom use.

IN CLASS

1 Ask the students to read the descriptions of the various zodiac signs which you have managed to find.

2 Ask them if they agree with the descriptions and whether they can add any information.

3 Ask them, working in groups, to allocate zodiac signs to the characters from their Reader based on their interpretations of what they have read.

TAURUS

Quiet, peace-loving, neat and tidy in appearance, loves to laugh, good entertaining company, cheerful, not faithful in relations with the opposite sex, free with money, often jealous.

GEMINI

Intelligent and thoughtful, a good talker and communicator, ambitious, a quick learner, curious about everything, a tale-teller, boastful, changeable.

CANCER

Soft and tender, a lover of honesty, moves house frequently, easily frightened, lives only for the present, peaceful, rather lazy, careless.

LEO

Faithful, needs to show power, wise, has good judgement, is hard-working, loves money, generous, affectionate, proud, restless, wasteful.

VIRGO

Intelligent and clever in discussion, clever with words, a lover of travel and foreign places, enjoys secrets, can make money easily, dishonest, pretends to know more than he does.

LIBRA

Quiet, does not enjoy quarrelling, pleasant, careful with his appearance, enjoys alcohol, often involved with romance, musical, not very hard-working, cheerful, does not take life very seriously.

SCORPIO

Brave and confident when in a fight, stubborn, proud of his reputation, likes to talk about himself, can be violent, does not make friends easily.

SAGITTARIUS

Generous, shy, faithful, loves to be fair, thinks of others as well as himself, fond of children, hates all wickedness, wise, can try too hard to make others like him.

CAPRICORN

A deep thinker, does not like to talk much, does not like to attract attention, patient and hard-working, enjoys study, worries a lot, can be jealous, does not trust others easily, can be hypocritical.

AQUARIUS

Prefers to listen rather than to speak, prepared to wait a long time for results to show, serious in argument, worries about others too much, rather serious in manner, a dreamer, lover of open spaces and freedom.

PISCES

Always sees the best in others, tries to do his best in all things, religious, enjoys conversation, puts the family first, very generous to others, can judge others badly, not very thoughtful, tries to make others like him.

ARIES

Courageous, a risk-taker, quarrelsome, dislikes authority, likes to talk about himself, wise when making decisions about himself, can be violent, can be deceitful.

COMMENT	This task can be performed in pairs or in groups and the choices they make should be justified with reference to episodes in the Reader. The vocabulary used in the table above may have to be modified to suit the level of the students.

2.4 Pick a pocket

LITERARY AIM	Reinterpretation and assessment of character through unusual perspective
LEVEL	Intermediate to Advanced
TIME	50–60 minutes
PREPARATION	You should prepare lists of items to use as examples and also be prepared to reveal what is in your own pocket and explain what it shows of character or life style.
IN CLASS	1 Ask the students if they agree that the contents of people's bags or pockets reveal something about character. Explain that often the police use the contents of the victim's pockets as their first clue when solving a crime.
	2 Ask the class to look at the contents of your pocket today and comment on what is revealed. The contents can be represented by a series of pictures.
	3 Next, ask them if they would be willing to empty their own pockets or handbags, or perhaps show the class one item which they think reveals something about their character or their way of life? Ask them to volunteer the information. Bear in mind that the activity works best if the teacher is also prepared to undergo the same treatment.
	4 Then ask them to consider what the characters in their Reader would carry around with them. If ideas are slow in coming, the following lists can provide a stimulus. Ask the students if any of these lists conjure up associations with the characters they have encountered in their reading. If not, ask them what associations they do conjure up and then in groups they should make their own lists for each character. Lists can be compared. Suggestions should be justified in some way: perhaps the item was specifically referred to in the Reader; or the item shows some aspect of personality; or the item is one which is associated with the character's profession or interests.
POCKET 1	three old newspaper weather maps a plastic bottle cap a new cork a pair of sunglasses

a tube of insect repellent
two unused Band Aids
loose matches
ten new pence

POCKET 2

two new buttons in a small envelope
a clean handkerchief
a used handkerchief
nail scissors
a comb
a small torch (working)
a pocket dictionary
£50 in new notes in a rubber band

2.5 Character zoo

LITERARY AIM

Reinterpretation and assessment of character through altered perspective

LEVEL

Elementary to Advanced

TIME

50 minutes

PREPARATION

Depending upon the level of the students you may find it helpful to prepare a list of animals and the characteristics or traits with which they are most usually associated. It is, however, much better if the students can provide this list of associations. (See the example checklist given at the end of this activity.)

IN CLASS

1 With a Reader such as *Animal Farm* (Longman) the obvious challenge is to see the animals as humans, but equally challenging is the attempt to see characters as animals. Treat the plot of the Reader as if it were a walk around a zoo. Give each character in the Reader the identity of an animal in the zoo according to the personality traits they exhibit, for example, courage = lion, stupidity = sheep.

2 This task may seem a little strange to the students at first, but if you provide a list of animals and birds with the characteristics for which they are best known the students will respond more readily. This list can be used as a checklist which will form the basis for discussion. Alternatively, the students can undertake to make this list before the discussion begins.

3 Ask the students to justify their choices, using illustration if possible, either with pictures from bird and animal books, or with drawings, depending on their willingness to draw.

Checklist

lion	brave, courageous, fierce
fox	cunning, sly, deceitful
pig	dirty, greedy
lamb	innocent, lively, gentle
elephant	good memory, strong
hare	mad, fast
mule	stubborn
mouse	quiet, timid
snail	slow
horse	strong, noble
owl	wise
cat	lazy, independent, curious
dog	faithful, friendly
sheep	stupid
peacock	proud
snake	evil, slippery, deceitful

3 Summarizing plot

3.1 Board games

LITERARY AIM

Selection, ordering, summarizing and assessment of events in visual format. Creative response to text

LEVEL

Elementary to Advanced

TIME

60 minutes preparing time
60 minutes playing time

INTRODUCTION

Once you have shown students how to play a board game based on a Reader they have just read they will enthusiastically create their own for subsequent books or stories.

The design of the board should reflect the theme or motif of the Reader, as shown in the example at the end of this activity. Board A is for 'The Courtship of Susan Bell', *Outstanding Short Stories* (Longman) where, as the story is primarily to do with love and marriage, a heart was used for the board. Board B is to accompany *The Thirty-Nine Steps* (Longman), in which Big Ben is one of the prime settings, and so a clock face was chosen for the board. Board C is for 'Lord Emsworth and the Girl Friend', *Outstanding Short Stories* (Longman), which deals with the planning of a path through the grounds of a stately home. Board C is an example of a student's work, and demonstrates the pains which some students take when making their own material. Students can work individually, or in groups to make games, but it is most effective if one student makes the board and another the quotation cards, while a third supplies the fact questions and a fourth checks the answers and writes them on the foot of each question card, or on a separate answer key sheet. When groups have completed their own games they can exchange material and play each other's games.

The board should have between twenty-four and thirty squares on it. Of these no more than three or four are left blank. The remaining squares are divided equally between questions and obstacles. Obstacle squares provide a small part of the storyline of the Reader which either encouraged, halted or delayed the action. Accordingly, the students are asked to move forwards, backwards or to wait and perhaps miss a turn. If they land on a question square they draw a card from a central pile of at least twenty cards, on which a question is written. The questions can be divided between Q questions and F questions, that is, between quotation questions and fact questions. The answers may also be written on these cards. However, if this is done the student's fellow players must read the questions aloud to avoid him reading the answer. They will also be able to tell him if his answer was correct, thereby minimizing your intervention in the activity.

Students play the game in groups of three or four; so sufficient copies of the board and the question cards must be made. The players move tokens around the board with the aid of a dice.

PREPARATION

If you are taking a board game into the class you will need one board, one dice, and one set of questions for every group of four students. If the students are making boards they will need one large piece of card, and paper for question cards for every group of four students.

IN CLASS

1 It may be necessary to explain the concept of a board game as not all foreign cultures are familiar with the principles. First of all, give out the boards and explain how the dice will tell each competitor how many squares they can move around the board. Explain that they will need some small token or object to move around the board and that every player moves a different token. Next, inform the students about the Q squares and explain that they have to get a question right if they want to leave the square again. Then, explain that some squares will give them some instructions which they must follow. Try to get the students to appreciate that the instructions correspond to the action in the Reader.

2 Distribute the cards and dice, check that all students have a token to move and allow them to begin playing. You act as monitor, adviser and referee while the game is taking place.

3 Students will probably move around the board quite swiftly, if the questions are easy and the board uncomplicated, so you may find it useful to say that the winner in each group is the student who has made the greatest number of complete circuits in an allotted time, rather than the first student to reach the final square.

Board A
'Courtship of Susan Bell'

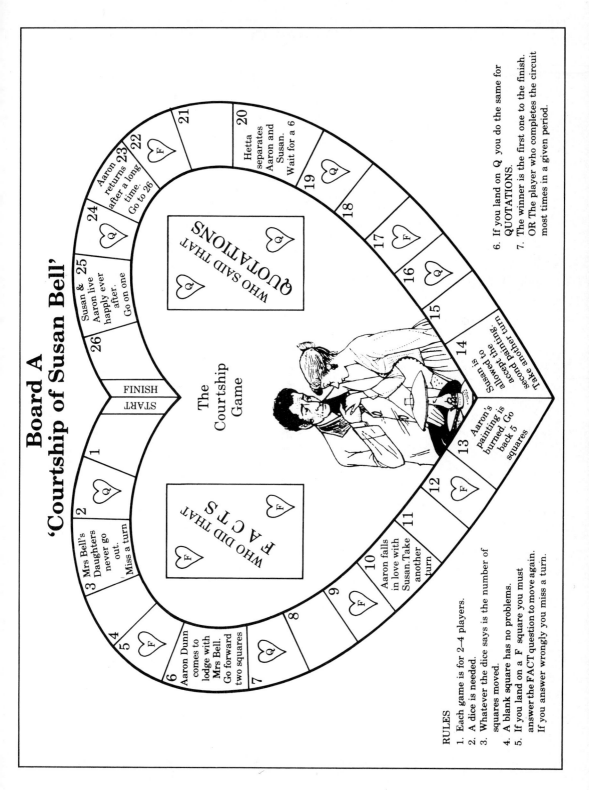

The Courtship Game

WHO DID THAT FACTS

WHO SAID THAT QUOTATIONS

START
FINISH

1

2 Q

3 Mrs Bell's Daughters never go out. Miss a turn.

4

5 F

6 Aaron Dunn comes to lodge with Mrs Bell. Go forward two squares

7 Q

8

9 F

10 Aaron falls in love with Susan. Take another turn

11

12 F

13 Aaron's painting is burned. Go back 5 squares

14 Susan is allowed to accept the painting. Take another turn.

15

16 Q

17 F

18

19 Q

20 Hetta separates Aaron and Susan. Wait for a 6

21

22 F

23 Aaron returns after a long time. Go to 26

24 Q

25 Q

26 Susan & Aaron live happily ever after. Go on one

RULES

1. Each game is for 2–4 players.
2. A dice is needed.
3. Whatever the dice says is the number of squares moved.
4. A blank square has no problems.
5. If you land on a F square you must answer the FACT question to move again. If you answer wrongly you miss a turn.
6. If you land on Q you do the same for QUOTATIONS.
7. The winner is the first one to the finish. OR The player who completes the circuit most times in a given period.

Board B

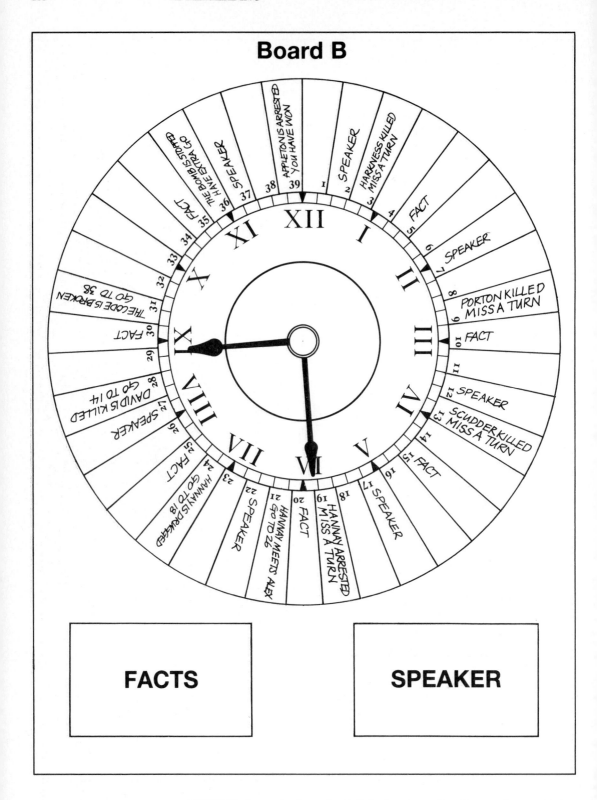

FACTS

SPEAKER

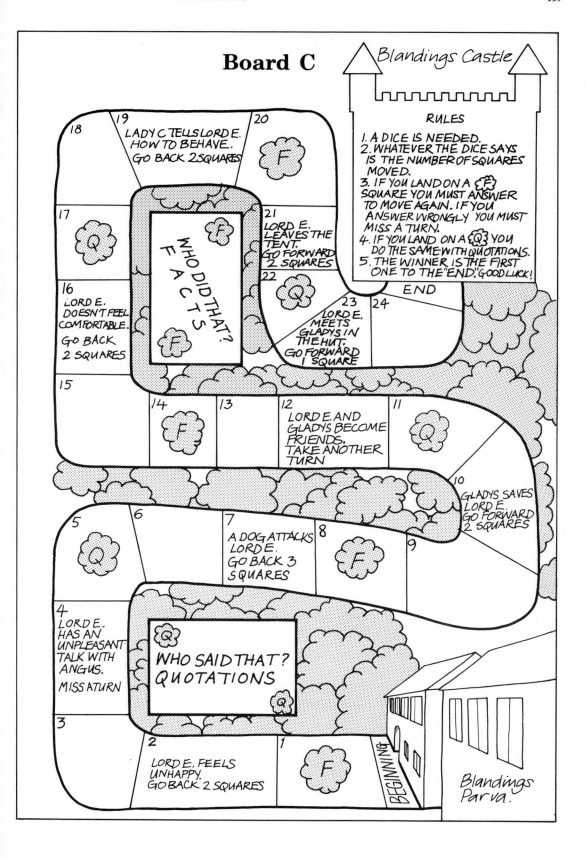

Board C

Blandings Castle

18 | 19 LADY C. TELLS LORD E. HOW TO BEHAVE. GO BACK 2 SQUARES | 20 F

RULES
1. A DICE IS NEEDED.
2. WHATEVER THE DICE SAYS IS THE NUMBER OF SQUARES MOVED.
3. IF YOU LAND ON A F SQUARE YOU MUST ANSWER TO MOVE AGAIN. IF YOU ANSWER WRONGLY YOU MUST MISS A TURN.
4. IF YOU LAND ON A Q YOU DO THE SAME WITH QUOTATIONS.
5. THE WINNER IS THE FIRST ONE TO THE "END". GOOD LUCK!

17 Q

WHO DID THAT? FACTS

21 LORD E. LEAVES THE TENT. GO FORWARD 2 SQUARES

16 LORD E. DOESN'T FEEL COMFORTABLE. GO BACK 2 SQUARES

22 Q

23 | 24 LORD E. MEETS GLADYS IN THE HUT. GO FORWARD 1 SQUARE

END

15

14 F | 13 | 12 LORD E. AND GLADYS BECOME FRIENDS. TAKE ANOTHER TURN | 11 Q

10 GLADYS SAVES LORD E. GO FORWARD 2 SQUARES

5 Q | 6 | 7 A DOG ATTACKS LORD E. GO BACK 3 SQUARES | 8 F | 9

4 LORD E. HAS AN UNPLEASANT TALK WITH ANGUS. MISS A TURN

WHO SAID THAT? QUOTATIONS

3 | 2 LORD E. FEELS UNHAPPY. GO BACK 2 SQUARES | 1 F

BEGINNING

Blandings Parva.

3.2 Documentary summaries

LITERARY AIM   Selection, ordering, interpreting and summarizing events and
their repercussions in a visual format. Creative response to text

LEVEL   Intermediate to Advanced

TIME   60 minutes

PREPARATION   If the students have already used documents prepared by you as a
pre-reading activity (see activity A2.4) they will have less trouble
producing their own. (See also the examples given at the end of this
activity.)

IN CLASS   1 If the idea is new to the students they will very quickly latch on
to the technique if they are first reminded of all the ways in which
we record information; from ticket stubs to grave stones. You
should also encourage them to suggest what probably happened if a
certain document exists; for example a grave stone suggests that one
of the characters died, a wedding invitation suggests that two of the
characters got married, and an entrance ticket implies that one of
the characters visited a certain building.

2 Ask the students to go back through the Reader and identify the
occasions when a document is mentioned, is implied, or could have
accompanied an event. You can write the list of their suggestions on
the board.

3 Students are then, individually or in groups, given responsibility
for producing a reasonable facsimile of one of the documents,
taking into account the age, ability, culture and experience of the
students. The documents are not necessarily produced to scale.

4 The final collection of documents is displayed for the class to see
and to serve as a brief reminder or summary of the Reader.

VARIATION   An alternative is to ask each individual student to summarize the
story in the form of ten documents. These do not have to be
produced in detail or show any artistic talent. Which ten documents
would they choose and why?

The following documents were produced for *The Thirty-Nine Steps*
(Longman). Students took great pains to suggest authenticity and
even deliberately stained and aged the map to imply that the bearer
of this map had suffered some hardship while carrying it.

3.3 Pictogram summaries

LITERARY AIM   Selection, ordering, summarizing, and interpreting events
                     and possible alternative structures

LEVEL   Intermediate to Advanced

TIME   45–60 minutes

INTRODUCTION   A summary does not have to take the form of sentences and
                     paragraphs. Nor does it have to be in written form at all. It can take
                     the form of a diagram or flow chart or combination of the two, that
                     is, a pictogram. Pictogram summarizing involves recording all the
                     choices open to the character throughout the story as well as the
                     course of action actually decided upon. It also makes students
                     appreciate the dynamics of plot construction and character
                     motivation.

PREPARATION

IN CLASS   1 Explain to the students that the plots of most Readers involve
                     characters making decisions which can affect the entire course of
                     the action. Characters are given choices to make and, within the
                     frame of the plot, they either choose to do one thing or the other,
                     notwithstanding authorial autocracy, of course.

                     2 Ask the students to make a list of the key events of the story.
                     Then ask them to consider what choices the main character had at
                     that stage. These can be listed too. Then, ask what would have
                     happened if the character had not made the choice he made.
                     Alternatives can also be listed. This also provides useful practice of
                     the third conditional along the way. Usually, if the character had
                     not chosen to act the way he did the story would have ground to a
                     halt.

                     The following example is for 'X-ing a Paragraph', *Outstanding Short
                     Stories* (Longman). Once students have seen an example of the
                     technique they can produce their own pictograms (or flow charts for
                     the non-artistic).

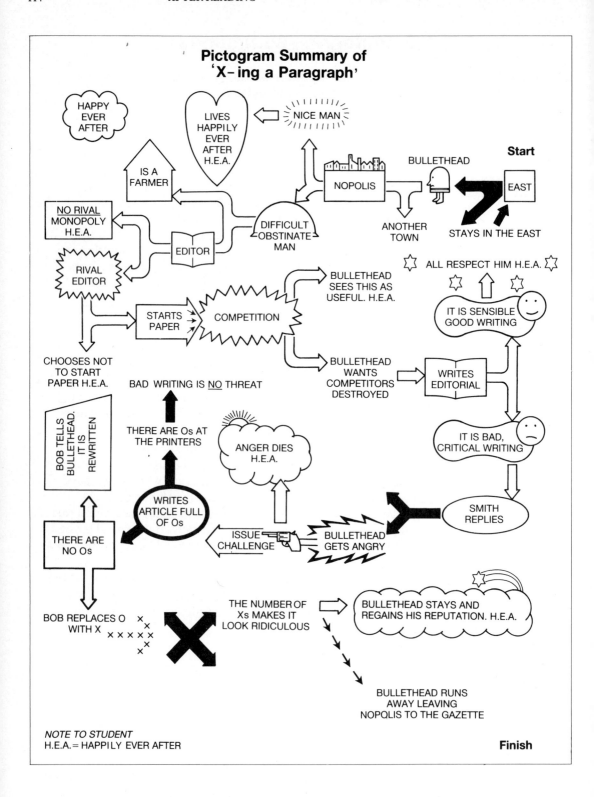

Pictogram Summary of 'X-ing a Paragraph'

HAPPY EVER AFTER

LIVES HAPPILY EVER AFTER H.E.A.

NICE MAN

BULLETHEAD

Start

IS A FARMER

NOPOLIS

EAST

NO RIVAL MONOPOLY H.E.A.

DIFFICULT OBSTINATE MAN

ANOTHER TOWN

STAYS IN THE EAST

EDITOR

RIVAL EDITOR

ALL RESPECT HIM H.E.A.

BULLETHEAD SEES THIS AS USEFUL. H.E.A.

STARTS PAPER

COMPETITION

IT IS SENSIBLE GOOD WRITING

CHOOSES NOT TO START PAPER H.E.A.

BAD WRITING IS NO THREAT

BULLETHEAD WANTS COMPETITORS DESTROYED

WRITES EDITORIAL

BOB TELLS BULLETHEAD. IT IS REWRITTEN

THERE ARE Os AT THE PRINTERS

ANGER DIES H.E.A.

IT IS BAD, CRITICAL WRITING

WRITES ARTICLE FULL OF Os

SMITH REPLIES

THERE ARE NO Os

ISSUE CHALLENGE

BULLETHEAD GETS ANGRY

BOB REPLACES O WITH X × × × × × × × × ×

THE NUMBER OF Xs MAKES IT LOOK RIDICULOUS

BULLETHEAD STAYS AND REGAINS HIS REPUTATION. H.E.A.

BULLETHEAD RUNS AWAY LEAVING NOPOLIS TO THE GAZETTE

NOTE TO STUDENT
H.E.A. = HAPPILY EVER AFTER

Finish

3.4 Reading by proxy

LITERARY AIM	**Interpretation and revision of plot and event**
LEVEL	**Intermediate to Advanced**
TIME	**15 minutes per conference**
INTRODUCTION	If books are in temporary short supply groups can be given responsibility for making a Reader come to life for the rest of the class.
PREPARATION	Try to have four or five copies of four Readers (A, B, C and D). Divide the class into four groups. Ask group A to read title A and so on. Give the groups a deadline by which they must all have completed their reading. The reading will be done outside the classroom, and so the books should not be too difficult for the students to read and enjoy alone.
IN CLASS	1 Explain to the class that the members of each group are to take on the roles of the key characters in their particular Reader. These characters are to hold a press conference for the rest of the class who have not read the book and will act as journalists trying to find out what happened. Before the conference the group must prepare a brief press release which will give their names and a very brief, bare description of what happened; for example, 'Involved in a hijack attempt which failed.'
	2 At the end of the interviews the journalists write up a report or article for the Reader(s) they have not read. The following day, week, or month, another group holds a press conference. If after the interview, any of the journalists are sufficiently curious to request another group's Reader for extensive reading for pleasure, so much the better. It has been found that knowledge of the outcome of the book does not necessarily dull the curiosity to read.

3.5 Picture gallery

LITERARY AIM	**Summarizing, ordering and interpreting text to visual cues and prompts**
LEVEL	**Elementary to Advanced**
TIME	**90 minutes**
INTRODUCTION	Occasionally, Readers are rich in illustrations. If a Reader at a more advanced level is rather sparsely illustrated it is suggested that the teacher seek out the edition for a lower level of ability and use the illustrations found there. For example, the Advanced level edition

of *Silas Marner* (Longman) had very little artwork, while an edition intended for the Intermediate level (Macmillan) was richly illustrated. About twenty different illustrations are needed for this activity.

PREPARATION

Mount the illustrations on card. Make sure that all references to page numbers are removed. If the illustrations are ludicrously small it is advisable, if possible, to enlarge them until they are all approximately A4 size.

IN CLASS

1 Distribute a few pictures at random to groups of three or four students. No group should have any picture which any other group has.

2 Ask the students first to identify the incident portrayed in each illustration. If they do recognize the episode, then ask them to write on the reverse of the picture a brief description of that episode. This need only be a single sentence.

3 When the students have labelled the pictures in this way allocate certain groups responsibility for different episodes in the Reader. This can merely be the beginning, the middle and the end if the plot is fairly straightforward. They may refer to the sentences written on the reverse of the drawing for help. Each group collects the illustrations which accompany their section.

4 When each group has their collection of pictures they should attempt to put them in chronological order. When they are happy with the order, information can be added to the illustrations according to comic strip convensions. Speech should be put into speech bubbles; thoughts should be put into thought bubbles; and extra information should be put inside balloon shapes at the top or bottom of the picture.

5 The students should then glue these additions to the pictures onto the illustrations, therefore the additions should not be too lengthy or they will cover most of the picture. The completed 'comic strip' version of the Reader can be turned into a frieze going around the room. This is particularly useful if other classes use the same room as they will benefit vicariously from the work of the original class.

COMMENT

This activity has proved to be a popular one as it stimulates a lot of discussion about the Reader, encourages revision, and involves the skills of selection, adaptation and summarizing.

4 Interpretive extensions and projects

4.1 By any other name

LITERARY AIM **Reassessment and interpretation of text, plot and theme**

LEVEL **Intermediate to Advanced**

TIME **60 minutes minimum**

INTRODUCTION This activity is a variation on the standard task of giving a Reader another title once it has been read.

PREPARATION You should prepare the task sheet below so that every student has a copy. The language may have to be simplified for use with Lower Intermediate level students.

IN CLASS 1 Give out copies of the task sheet.
2 Ask the students either as individuals, or in groups, to fill in the task sheet.

FIND...
1 An existing song title which would make a good title for the Reader.

2 An existing book title which would make a good alternative title for the Reader.

3 An existing film title which would make a good alternative title for the Reader.

4 A line or phrase from poetry or rhyme which would make a good alternative title for the Reader.

5 A perfume, aftershave, or cosmetic which would make a good title for the Reader.

6 A quotation from the Reader itself which could provide a good title.

7 A proverb or motto which could be a good title.

8 An alliterative title of three words; that is, all three words should begin with the same letter.

NOTE: You may make photocopies of this for classroom use (but please note that copyright law does not normally permit multiple copying of published material).

3 When the task sheet has been completed, put the students into four groups and ask them to decide on one title for each category. When their selection of thirty-two titles has been narrowed down to eight, regroup the four groups so that four different lists are debated again. This process of narrowing down by discussion can be continued until each group has only one title.

4.2 Project work

LITERARY AIM	**Extension of theme, motif, plot**
LEVEL	**Elementary to Advanced**
TIME	**2/3 lessons**
PREPARATION	None.

IN CLASS

A project should involve the students doing research, finding or creating illustrations, reporting information from experts and giving their own views. It can, and should, be displayed as a class effort with individual contributions being credited.

The chosen project can culminate in a Reader or the chosen Reader can initiate a project. *The Poseidon Adventure* (OUP), for example, can generate a large-scale project covering areas such as:

1 Ships (categories, famous ones)
2 Disasters at sea (the Titanic)
3 Holidays at sea (what do the brochures offer?)
4 The Greek Islands (what to see and do, an itinerary)

Hijacked (OUP), could lead to projects along similar lines:

1 Aircraft (types of passenger aircraft)
2 Hijacking (a study of press cuttings)
3 Airports and airlines
4 History of flight
5 The job of the air traffic controller, pilot, steward(ess)
6 Emergency procedure in a plane

4.3 Now and then

LITERARY AIM	**Imaginative interpretation and extension of theme and plot**
LEVEL	**Elementary to Advanced**
TIME	**45–60 minutes**
PREPARATION	None.

IN CLASS

1 If, after reading is completed, interest in the plot and theme of a Reader are still relatively high, students often find it stimulating to shift perspective to a time, place, or culture which are completely different to those found in the Reader, but which still allow the story to 'work'.

2 For example, *The Piper of Hamelin* (OUP) can become the story of a rock musician; and *Animal Farm* (Longman) can be transposed to a toy shop, or to a language school where the students throw out the owner and run the school themselves. The students could write down the transposed story or simply use it as the basis for discussion.

COMMENT

The story of a Reader does not always strike a student as being universally relevant. Transposition can bring the theme to life still more and can increase identification with characters in their various predicaments.

4.4 Silent film

LITERARY AIM

Imaginative reinterpretation and extension of text

LEVEL

Elementary to Advanced

TIME

3–4 hours (not continuous)

INTRODUCTION

A teacher sometimes finds that a class of students is initially too shy either to move or speak when dramatizing a story. However, despite this reluctance they demonstrate curiosity about interpretive work. The 'Silent Film' technique can break the ice for students who are secretly longing to 'have a go' at drama, but need a little encouragement and confidence-building first. (See *Drama* by Charlyn Wessels (1987) in this series.)

PREPARATION

None.

IN CLASS

1 The story of the film must first be broken down into twenty-four or thirty-six tableaux. These numbers are not arbitrary; they refer to the type of photographic film at your disposal. The tableaux must correspond to the twenty-four or thirty-six most important or necessary scenes in the Reader. If the students have trouble grasping this concept suggest to them that a famous painter is thinking about painting twenty-four paintings to tell the story of their Reader. Ask them which scenes they think the painter should choose. A great deal of discussion and argument can be generated by this initial selection.

2 Allocate the students to the roles of the characters in the Reader. The students should design and present each tableau, which should then be photographed, either by you or a team of students. The students who are not in the photograph should direct (or assist with property and costume, if required). To accompany each 'still' the students should make a card explaining the action and perhaps providing dialogue in the way that such cards use to provide dialogue for the audiences who went to view the old silent films.

3 Depending on the enthusiasm of the class the project can grow to include make-up and masks, and location shots can be attempted if appropriate. If the film is then developed as a series of slides the completed 'Silent Film' can be shown first to the class which created it and then to other classes.

4 The amount of language used in the presentation is simply that found on the twenty-four or thirty-six cards. However, the language generated in the organization and development of the whole project is rich and varied.

If the students' confidence increases as a result of this 'frozen' drama, then subsequent projects including movement and slides could be replaced with video, if this is at the disposal of the teacher.

COMMENT

It is my experience that science fiction stories go down extremely well with younger classes and the scope for mask-making projects and imaginative costume-making is wider. A class of thirteen year-olds who had previously not been enjoying an adaption of H.G. Wells' *First Men on the Moon* (Longman), thoroughly enjoyed the challenge of providing their own interpretation of the story in this way.

4.5 Puppets

LITERARY AIM

Imaginative reinterpretation and extension of text

LEVEL

Intermediate to Advanced

TIME

3–4 hours (not continuous)

INTRODUCTION

A similar, but much more ambitious, project can be attempted with puppets. Some years ago a class of reluctant readers were encouraged to read *Animal Farm* (Longman), with the challenge of adapting it to a script for puppets which they had made. The final performance was given to a class of younger students.

PREPARATION

For the theatre you will need a large cardboard box with slits cut down the sides to allow the entrance and exit of the puppet characters. The puppets do not need any working parts and can be merely two-dimensional drawings made by some of the more artistic students. Attach the drawings to long rods. They can enter the stage via the slits at the sides.

IN CLASS

1 Ask the students to divide the Reader into five acts. Ask them to take responsibility for selecting, and where necessary editing, important dialogue and, when appropriate, providing a part for a narrator.

2 Give the final 'script' to the students to rehearse and if you wish record on to cassette.

3 When the students are confident with the script put on the performance.

4 Make the students who will be manipulating the puppets know they must listen carefully and follow the taped script in order not to miss cues.

5 Reviewing and recommending

5.1 Read this!

LITERARY AIM   Critical appraisal and recommendation to others

LEVEL   Intermediate to Advanced

TIME   60–120 minutes

INTRODUCTION   Class sets of Readers can be in short supply at the start of term, for financial or other reasons, or the teacher may wish the process of book selection to be the responsibility of the students. The temporary lack of a class set of Readers, whether self-imposed or enforced, can be turned to advantage.

PREPARATION   None.

IN CLASS   1 Divide the class into groups of three or four and allocate each group the responsibility of, first, selecting a Reader from those five or six which are available, from publishers' catalogues, or the remains of last year's class library.

2 The students should all read the book by an agreed deadline.

3 They must then plan an election or a sales pitch campaign. The object of this campaign is to persuade other students of their own level to select their book as one of the class Readers.

4 The campaign can take any form; for example, posters, slogans or a speech. This works best if two teachers with two classes of the same level can get involved. The two classes should be brought together on the day of the campaigns and then vote for the three books which sound the most interesting. Students from class A1 will mount a campaign for students in class A2 and vice versa. The beauty of this activity is that, as well as the students deciding which books they will use for intensive reading (which is useful for motivation), extensive reading is necessary before mounting the campaign, and can be encouraged afterwards if students are curious about the books which were not chosen as class Readers.

5.2 Will/Did I enjoy it?

LITERARY AIM   **Critical appraisal and assessment of students' reading habits**

LEVEL   **Intermediate to Advanced**

TIME   **45–60 minutes**

PREPARATION   At the start of the year a questionnaire can be designed by you or the students to determine whether or not they like to read, and if so, why and what. (See the example given at the end of this activity which may be copied for classroom use.)

IN CLASS   1 Once the questionnaire is designed the students should circulate around the class and ask other students the questions on it. If they were to sit by themselves in silence filling in the questionnaire, there would be no interaction about the topic. The questionnaire should be written so that the students have to invent the questions.
2 The feedback for this can be done in small groups, or as a class. Questions asked at this stage can help you to plan and select material more appropriately for the level, interests and personality of the class.

Questionnaire—Part A

1 Find a student who has read a novel, in any language, for enjoyment during the past four weeks.

Name ------------------------------   What s/he read ------------------------------

2 Find a student who doesn't have time to read for pleasure.

Name ------------------------------   Reason ------------------------------

3 Find a student who has bought a book or magazine written in English in the last four weeks.

Name ------------------------------   Title ------------------------------

4 Find a student who has read a book in English which s/he really enjoyed in the last year.

Name ------------------------------   Leading Character ------------------------------

5 Find a student who has read and not enjoyed a book in English in the previous year.

Name ------------------------------   Title ------------------------------

6 Find a student who has a favourite author and who has read as much of that author as possible. The author does not have to be English.

Name ------------------------------   Author ------------------------------

7 Find a student who enjoys reading a certain type of book; for example, romance, espionage, autobiographies, etc. This does not have to be in English.

Name ------------------------------   Type ------------------------------

8 Interview one student and ask how many of the following s/he agrees with.

Put + + for strong agreement
Put +   for agreement
Put −   for disagreement
Put − − for strong disagreement

Reading is one of my favourite pastimes. ☐

Reading is OK if there is nothing else to do. ☐

I only like reading in English if the language is made simple. ☐

I don't like reading simplified books because it spoils them. ☐

I like books to have a good story-line. ☐

I prefer short stories because I get bored/tired easily. ☐

I do not like to give my opinion about what I've read. ☐

I like someone to translate the words I do not understand. ☐

I prefer one long story to several short stories. ☐

I do not like books to have pictures. It is childish. ☐

Pictures help me to understand. I like them. ☐

I read a lot at work/school. Reading is no fun! ☐

I read for fun/pleasure in my own language, but not in English. ☐

I like to read, but I am not a literature student; so don't ask my opinion. ☐

Questionnaire—Part B

To be completed after a book has been read.

1 Find a student who enjoyed this book.

Name   -------------------------------   How much? (scale 1–10)   -------------

2 Find a student who didn't enjoy this book .

Name   -------------------------------   Why   ---------------------------------

----

3 Find a student who would like to change the look of the book. What would they alter; for example, cover illustrations, print?

Name   -------------------------------   How would you change it?   ----------------

----

4 In your partner's opinion who was the most interesting character?

----

5 In your partner's opinion who was the funniest character?

----

6 Which incident or episode does your partner think was the most

interesting?   --

exciting? ---

moving? --

amusing?   ---

7 Which character reminded your partner most of him or herself, and of you?

Name   -------------------------------   Character   ----------------------------

8 Would your partner recommend this book to another student to read?

Who?   --

9 Do you think that (student's name) ----------------------- in this group enjoyed this story? Do not ask this student. Try to guess.

10 Would your partner read another book by this author?

----

11 Has anyone read another book by this author?

Title ---

Section D
Changing frame

Changing frame

Introduction

Students are frequently asked to read only as students; we ask them to read and answer questions afterwards. Yet reading for pleasure is frequently done in role. We read in a variety of roles which increase our interest, pleasure and involvement: for example, roles such as spouses, teachers, travellers, day-dreamers, patients, and only occasionally as students. Reading professionally brings in other roles again: the book critic would read a book in a very different way from a student. Knowing this, we should be encouraging this role recognition and development in our classes, but we often restrict entry into these 'inner worlds' by insisting on narrow, language-based tasks only; tasks which reinforce the role of the student, and reduce the risk involved in imaginative response to writing. For there *is* a risk; the teacher is no longer solely the teacher, but is also involved in the affective task rather than controlling a cognitive one.

Changing frame need not be traumatic for the student, or the teacher. It can and should be done gently. You are not asking students to read in a false role, that is, by giving them a false identity (for example, you are Joe Smith, a 35 year-old father of two, and an astronaut). You are asking them to remain as themselves, but to look at what they are reading with some other aspect of their persona to the fore. Language becomes the medium for expressing this aspect, rather than an end in itself.

This change of perspective or frame can alter the way students view plot, theme and event and, thereby, alters the language the students use to describe them. It is possible for students to read an entire Reader in frame, or for the frame to be introduced during the reading to enable the student to view an incident from another perspective.

Framed discussion

For example, the story of *Silas Marner* (Macmillan) includes the arrival of the two year-old child Eppie into the life of Silas. It is possible for the class to view this from the perspective of an adoption committee comprising three groups of social workers.

In class each group can put forward a case for granting adoption to one of three characters: Silas who is old, lonely and infirm; Dolly who is a good, but poor woman from the village with a large family of her own; and Godfrey who is the child's real father, and is rich and irresponsible. While they are putting forward their own case for adoption they should try to discredit the cases put forward by the other groups. They can use the text itself as evidence to support their arguments if necessary. After the hearing a secret ballot is taken and custody is awarded. They then read on to see if their choice was wise and if it was the same choice as that of the author. During the hearing, their language is controlled by you and also the frame. You are also in role as the chairperson of the hearing and are, therefore, providing a language role model for the students to follow.

Using other possible frames

The problem page (activity A4.2) is one of the easier methods of frame-changing. Another way is to make the class a community or group which share closeness, fears, superstitions, habits and an established hierarchy. Communities can be very loosely interpreted to include travellers on a journey, members of a jury, a staff room of teachers, a company of workers, or a group of advisers.

Introduction of the new frame can take place before reading so that the entire story includes the student as participant as well as observer. This can be done with very simple Readers such as the *Poseidon Adventure* (OUP), or at Intermediate level with, for example, *Hijacked* (OUP). Part of the success of changing frame is to establish a brief history for the new frame. This can be done most simply with a brief series of questions for which any answers are possible within the new frame.

Pre-questions to put students into frame

Poseidon Adventure

1 What is your reason for travelling?
2 Where is your cabin? Describe it.
3 What do you want to do on the voyage?
4 Who is meeting you, if anybody?

Hijacked

1 What is your reason for travelling?
2 Where are you sitting? Why?
3 What luggage do you have?
4 Who is meeting you and who saw you off, if anyone?
5 How do you intend to spend the journey?

Silas Marner

1 How long have you lived in this community?
2 Describe an average day.
3 Who are your closest friends?
4 What do you fear most in your community?
5 What superstitions do you have?
6 How do you feel about strangers coming to live here?

Writing summaries in frame

Framed summaries are also possible after the Reader has been read and discussed. The students are not only writing as students but within the frame of the story.

Framed summaries

For example, the short story 'Lord Mountdrago', *Outstanding Short Stories* (Longman) can be summarized as follows (Figure 1) within the frame of a medical report, and group efforts can be typed by you or the students, to make them more authentic if required. (The example may be copied for classroom use.)

Mountdrago	
1st Appointment 5.30p.m.	Reluctant. Late, very aggressive. Aware of position. Very anxious. Looked tired. Defensive. Bad dreams. Humiliation and embarrasment. 1. Underwear at state occasion .... laughter 2. Song instead of speech .... laughter 3. Caught in bar with low women .... violence All dreams include an Owen Griffiths. Troubled by coincidences after dreams. Fears judgement. Suppressed sexuality and violence perhaps? Trouble with father? Hatred of Welsh? Reluctant truth. Dreams 3 weeks. Insomnia - work. Threats of violence in desperation. Has medicine from doctor... prescribed rest. Competitive instincts..aggression to O.G... guilt. Parental presence.... much guilt.
Further visits	Temper declining. Need to talk freely. Dreams worsening, Exhaustion. Affecting concentration. No signs of improvement.
Penultimate visit	Hypnosis, initially successful. Resistance. Rejected. Refusal to apologise - anger extreme - silence for several minutes - apologised. Refused to cooperate. Left early.
Ultimate visit 6p.m. Dr. Audlin	Late - appointment cancelled. Considered possibility of L.M. stopping work. Going to suggest to Foreign Office. News of suicide a shock but always likely. Owen G.'s death more surprising. Coincidence alarming. UNSOLVED.

Figure 1

NOTE: You may make photocopies of this for classroom use (but please note that copyright law does not normally permit multiple copying of published material).

Horoscopes can present another example of framed summary (see activity A2.2). If students have been exposed to examples which you have produced as a pre-reading activity they will more readily adapt to summarizing a plot as a series of horoscope forecasts which came true.

The following example of the same story – 'Lord Mountdrago' – has also been summarized as a series of four horoscope forecasts. (See figure 2, which may be copied for Classroom use.)

LEO 10th
You take your power, responsibilities in your stride. But lately your over-active imagination has caused problems and you have neglected your health. A new acquaintance will have a relaxing effect on you. Share your problem.

LEO 17th
Anxiety is affecting sleep this month. Worries will affect work today and for a while to come. Take things more in your stride and seek further advice from others. Do not be too proud to seek help even if you feel foolish.

LEO 24th
Your usual confidence is in the decline today and Leo aggression is directed at an old rival. This rivalry will cause more problems if peace is not made soon. Try not to panic about the future.

LEO 31st
Violence today! Try to control the black feelings of despair. You will be at an all time low. Don't let the future worry you. Do something definite to remove problems. Later in the day will be very peaceful.

AQUARIUS 10th
Today is a demanding day professionally. You will have many opportunities to help others and use your gifts. A new acquaintance will prove difficult but persevere and a tragedy will be avoided. Secrets will be shared today.

AQUARIUS 17th
Your patience will be sorely tried today. Someone in trouble needs your help. Try to be more imaginative and understanding. Do not dismiss the impossible too easily. You will have trouble understanding others today.

AQUARIUS 24th
You go too far to patch up another's problems and quarrels. Stay calm when help is rejected. Try not to get too involved with the future plans of others. Violence will enter your day indirectly.

AQUARIUS 31st
Be prepared for bad news about public figures in your circle of acquaintances. An unsolved problem will worry you and appointments will be cancelled. A sad day.

Figure 2

Report writing in frame

Another example of framed writing is to view and report on a character as a psychoanalyst would. This can be done at any stage during the reading and does not have to be saved until the end.

Framed report writing

For example, when reading *Silas Marner* (Macmillan) students were asked to answer the following questionnaire on behalf of the character Silas. The questionnaire itself is authentic and is taken from an article on stress in society and how to avoid it. (See figure 3.)

How Vulnerable are you to Stress?
The following test was developed by psychologists Lyle H. Miller and Alma Dell Smith at the Boston Medical Centre. Score each item from 1(almost always), 2 (often), 3 (sometimes), 4 (rarely) to 5 (never), according to how much of the time it applies.

A I eat at least one hot balanced meal a day.

B I get seven to eight hours sleep a night.

C I give and receive affection often.

D I have at least one relative within 100 km. on whom I can rely.

E I exercise to the point of perspiration at least twice a week.

F I smoke less than half a packet of cigarettes a day.

G I take fewer than five alcoholic drinks a week.

H I am the correct weight for my height.

I I have an income adequate for basic expenses.

J I get strength from my religious beliefs.

K I regularly attend social activities.

L I have a network of close friends.

M I have one or more friends to confide in on personal matters.

N I am in good health.

O I am able to speak openly about my feelings when angry or worried.

P I have regular conversations with people I live with about domestic problems.

Q I do something for fun at least once a week.

R I am able to organize my time efficiently.

S I drink fewer than 3 cups of coffee a day.

T I take some quiet time to myself every day.

Total
Add up each score out of 5. Take away 20 from the total. Anything over 30 shows vulnerability to stress. 50-75 means serious vulnerability. Over 75 is an extremely dangerous vulnerability to stress.

Figure 3

In class, as a result of their findings and their perusal of Silas' case history which comprised relevant snippets from the first five chapters, a medical report was completed with the following headings to provide guidance:

Patient's name
Age
Occupation
Attitude to present society
Past experiences
Exercise taken
Diet
Health and general well-being
Obsessive behaviour
Observations, recommendations and warnings
Name of Doctor

Other useful frames

Useful frames which involve tasks which are both affective and cognitive are:

Psychiatrists
Policemen and detectives
Worried parents
Social workers
Problem page writers
Sensation-seeking journalists
Consumer researchers
Doctors
Film producers
Literature examiners
Museum curators
Artists and sculptors
Advertising and publishing firms
Toy manufacturers
Tee-shirt slogan writers

Section E
Scheme of work

Scheme of work

MATERIAL	'Lord Mountdrago' a story by W. Somerset Maugham from *Outstanding Short Stories* (see Appendix for synopsis).
LEVEL	2000 Headwords. Suitable for Upper Intermediate and Advanced.
LESSONS	50 minutes available.

Lesson	Suggested activities	See page	Time (minutes)
1	Picture Discussion	135	30 minutes
2	Role Play around the Picture	136	50 minutes
3	Problem-Solving with Horoscopes	137 also Section D	50 minutes
4	Extracts for Listening	138	30 minutes
5	Character Interpretation while Reading	140	50 minutes
6	Summarizing in Frame	142 also Section D	50 minutes
7	Summarizing in Frame	142 also Section D	50 minutes
8	Writing	142	50 minutes

However, not all of the lesson has to be devoted to the Reader. In lesson 4, for example, only 30 minutes is suggested for the activity. The actual reading itself could be begun in class after this activity and finished at home or in another lesson. The activities are in sequential order and while some activities can be omitted – it is not recommended that the order is changed. There is no hard and fast rule about how many activities are necessary. Lesson 2 could easily prove to be superfluous; while after reading lessons 7 and 8 could prove interchangeable.

Lesson 1

Picture Discussion

Lesson 2

Role Play around the Picture

FOR THE STUDENT   **1**

---
1 Decide who the two men in the picture are.
2 Decide why you are in the office.
3 Begin your role-playing with a customary greeting such as 'Hello' or 'Good Evening' and carry on from there.

Or   **2**

---
1 Take the roles your teacher gives you.
2 *You* decide why you are in the office.
3 Begin the role-playing with a customary greeting.

Or   **3**

---
1 Decide who the two men in the office are.
2 Take the reason given to you by the teacher as to why you are in the office.
3 Begin the role-playing with a customary greeting.

Or   **4**

---
1 Decide who the two men in the office are.
2 Decide why they are in the office.
3 Begin with one of the greetings supplied by the teacher.

FOR THE TEACHER   Teacher's suggestions   **1**

Two brothers	Boss and former employee
Doctor and patient	King and Prime Minister
Teacher and parent	Spy and his chief
Policeman and businessman	The Devil and a sinner
Two fathers	Lawyer and client
An actor and agent	Two rivals

Teacher's suggestions   **2**

To make a complaint	To give information
To meet after many years	To make an offer
To ask for money	To offer advice
To prove something illegal	To borrow something unusual
To hear the results of a will	To talk of their children
To break bad news	To make friends after a quarrel

Teacher's suggestions **3**

'Well I never!'	'How dare you!'
'So we meet again!'	'You are the only man I can turn to.'
'Congratulations!'	
'May I extend my sympathy.'	'I suppose you've read the papers.'
'Good grief. Did anyone see you?'	
	'I never expected to see *you* again.'
'So you changed your mind after all!'	
	'This is very serious!'
'May I introduce myself . . .'	
'I never forget a face.'	

Lesson 3

Problem-Solving with Horoscopes

FOR THE STUDENT   The horoscopes referred to are already available in Section D. Please see Framed Summaries, figure 2.

FOR THE TEACHER   *Suggestions*

1 Tell the students to read the horoscopes for homework the night before the lesson and to arrive with ideas for a story based only on the horoscopes.

or

2 Tell them to skim the horoscopes there and then in the lesson.

3 Read the information at the top of the student's page.

4 *Listen* to hypothetical plots. Try not to comment on how close they are to the truth.

5 After three minutes feed in the first piece of information; that 'Leo' is a Lord Mountdrago and 'Aquarius' is a Doctor Audlin. Allow the students to hypothesize further.

6 After three minutes feed in the second piece of information; that Lord Mountdrago is an important politician and that Doctor Audlin is a psychiatrist.

7 After a further three minutes of ideas feed in that Lord Mountdrago has problems with dreams and Doctor Audlin is famous for his understanding.

8 You must remember that no answer is wrong at this stage. Accept any interpretation as the student will be anxious to check his ideas against the real outcome.

Lesson 4

Extracts for Listening

Part one
Fill in the details on this medical card.

Name of patient _____

Age: _____   Marital Status: Married ☐ Single ☐

Family _____

Length of Marriage _____

Current Position _____

Family Doctor _____

Do you smoke?   Yes ☐   No ☐

Do you drink?   Yes ☐   No ☐

Do you do regular exercise? No ☐   Yes ☐

Are you in good health? (Tick box applicable.)

Satisfactory ☐   Poor ☐   Excellent ☐

Doctor consulted now _____

Part two
Tick whether these statements are *True* or *False*

		T	F
1	He has had more than one dream.	☐	☐
2	He was wearing his decorations to the party.	☐	☐
3	Owen Griffiths is from the Welsh Houses of Parliament.	☐	☐
4	He is excited by Lydia's guest list.	☐	☐
5	He suggests that the doctor wouldn't be welcome at one of these parties.	☐	☐
6	The only good feature of the house is the staircase.	☐	☐
7	Lady Connemara's ancestors were well-behaved.	☐	☐
8	He particularly wants to meet the Austrian Duke.	☐	☐
9	There is silence when royalty arrives.	☐	☐
10	He is dressed in short silk underwear.	☐	☐

Part three
Choose the right answers from those suggested below. Tick the boxes
of the items mentioned in the extract.

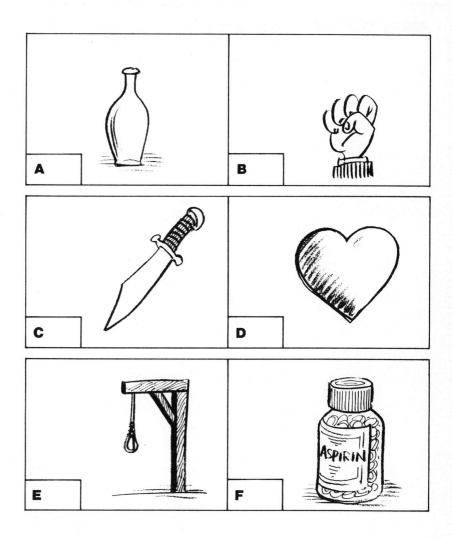

FOR THE TEACHER   The extracts for the listening are:

a from page 98:   'It seems it is exceedingly difficult to see you.'
    to page 101:   '. . . think me childish to come and see you.'
b from page 102: 'Well the first I had was about a month ago.'
    to page 103:   '. . . to find it was only a dream.'

Lesson 5

Character Interpretation while Reading

FOR THE STUDENT   Here is information from the story about Lord Mountdrago and Dr Audlin. Beside each fact say whether it refers to Lord Mountdrago M or Dr Audlin A or both B

- ☐ 1 Psychoanalyst
- ☐ 2 Exercises regularly
- ☐ 3 Wishes to be great
- ☐ 4 Sense of duty
- ☐ 5 Patient and calm
- ☐ 6 Pale, lined face
- ☐ 7 Good-looking
- ☐ 8 Has two sons
- ☐ 9 Went to Oxford University
- ☐ 10 Persistent
- ☐ 11 Unpopular and friendless
- ☐ 12 Lacks patience with others
- ☐ 13 Extremely patriotic
- ☐ 14 Expressionless eyes
- ☐ 15 Tall and thin
- ☐ 16 Tall and big
- ☐ 17 Good public speaker
- ☐ 18 Successful politician
- ☐ 19 Helped soldiers in war
- ☐ 20 Narrow-framed
- ☐ 21 Rather too fat
- ☐ 22 Works hard
- ☐ 23 Courageous
- ☐ 24 Arrogant
- ☐ 25 Aware of his cleverness
- ☐ 26 Rude to inferiors
- ☐ 27 Looks ill
- ☐ 28 Wears dark clothes
- ☐ 29 In perfect health
- ☐ 30 Speaks several languages
- ☐ 31 Studied in Vienna
- ☐ 32 Enjoys his work
- ☐ 33 Determined and ruthless
- ☐ 34 Slow musical voice
- ☐ 35 Underestimates his talent
- ☐ 36 Rich enough to retire
- ☐ 37 Rarely laughs
- ☐ 38 Finds apology difficult
- ☐ 39 Extremely snobbish
- ☐ 40 Not easily shocked
- ☐ 41 Slow to judge others
- ☐ 42 Inconsistent behaviour
- ☐ 43 Great self-control
- ☐ 44 Large, blue, tired eyes
- ☐ 45 Forty-two years-old
- ☐ 46 Consistent behaviour
- ☐ 47 Easily angered
- ☐ 48 Likes to be indispensible
- ☐ 49 Strong guilt complex
- ☐ 50 No more than fifty
- ☐ 51 Charges high fees
- ☐ 52 Married eighteen years
- ☐ 53 Selfish
- ☐ 54 Charming to friends
- ☐ 55 Dislikes failing somebody
- ☐ 56 Not interested in other women
- ☐ 57 Large, firm, cool hands
- ☐ 58 Can spot a liar
- ☐ 59 Excellent reputation
- ☐ 60 Has a soothing touch
- ☐ 61 Makes others fear him
- ☐ 62 Has knowledge of other countries
- ☐ 63 Grey, thinning hair
- ☐ 64 Aristocratic bearing
- ☐ 65 Smokes a little
- ☐ 66 Has many enemies
- ☐ 67 A hard judge of others
- ☐ 68 Honest
- ☐ 69 Greying hair
- ☐ 70 Private and public life are without fault
- ☐ 71 Looks much older
- ☐ 72 Makes others relax
- ☐ 73 Expression of pride
- ☐ 74 Not easily fooled
- ☐ 75 Is a gentleman

FOR THE TEACHER The students fill in the checklist while they are reading. The actual reading can take place in the classroom or at home.

After the checklist is completed ask the students to categorize it in three columns—A, M and B.

Once students have completed the exercise ask them to categorize the facts under the three headings below for each man.

PHYSICAL ATTRIBUTES			EXPERIENCE AND ACHIEVEMENTS			PERSONALITY		
A		**M**	**A**	**M**		**A**		**M**
6	60	7	1	2		5	72	3 38 70
14	63	16	19	8		10	74	4 39
15	71	21	31	9		35		11 42
20		29	51	17		37		12 47
27		45		18		40		13 48
28		64		30		41		23 49
34		69		52		43		24 53
44		73		65		46		25 54
50				66		55		26 56
57						58		33 67

BOTH	BOTH	BOTH
	22, 32, 36, 59, 62, 75	68

A further exercise is possible of categorizing essentials of character for this story. Ask students to draw a twelve-armed clock diagram either individually or in groups.

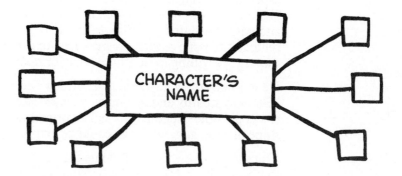

Students must then select the twelve *most* important points about each character, and put the number of that point into the box provided.

Lessons 6 and 7

Summarizing in Frame

FOR THE TEACHER   The stress report summary can be found in Section D. Please see Framed summaries, figure 3. The medical report is also in Section D, Framed summaries, figure 1.

Lesson 8

Writing

FOR THE STUDENT   **Task one**
Write a description of 'The Most Pleasant Man I've Ever Met'. Base your description on the antithesis of Lord Mountdrago which is found on page 96 ('Lord Mountdrago had many good qualities') to page 97 of the story ('. . . and was quite able to insult you again'). Do not follow the construction exactly and change anything which cannot be expressed sensibly in the opposite way.

FOR THE TEACHER   **Task one**
The passage does not have to be followed exactly, but it does provide a useful model.

'<u>James Meredith had many faults. He was not very bright and was lazy. He was inarticulate and had little experience of the world.</u>' He was weak and indecisive and was too shy to speak in public. He was a short, plain man, perhaps rather too thin. There was indeed a great deal about him which could make him unpopular and a failure. Fortunately he possessed great virtues.

He was very humble. He was extremely polite to everybody, especially servants. The lower officials all respected and liked him. He knew he was often less well informed than those he worked with and never hesitated to praise them. He was extremely patient and reluctant to issue orders. He preferred to listen to argument and was always willing to supply reasons for his actions.

He was extremely unselfish and had few enemies. He never refused help or sympathy and had many friends. Because of these qualities it was possible to endure his lack of organization and his failure to shine in company, where he could be extremely boring.

You should stress to the students that not every part of the extract can be neatly reversed. Paraphrasing is preferable to simply using the negative form of the verb. Perhaps it would be useful to offer those items underlined as a model or even as the introductory words to the composition.

FOR THE STUDENT   **Task two**
Write the newspaper reports which Dr Audlin reads on pages 115 and 116 of the story. Try to include everything that is mentioned in the author's account of these articles. Then enlarge this with your imagination.

FOR THE TEACHER   **Task two**
Find at least five students to write this composition. The stories can be a mixture of fact from the set book and imagination.

1 Prepare a newspaper front-page for the five students.

2 Divide the page into five large articles and five small ones that piece together to make the complete page. Cut the page into pieces to give to each student.

3 Each student should have one large article to write and one small one. They should supply their own headlines (and illustrations if they wish).

4 You should glue the finished articles onto the newspaper-layout. To avoid repetition you could ask each student to view the report from one point of view.

For example:

1 General news coverage.
2 Interviews with family.
3 The reaction of Parliament.
4 The reaction of witnesses.
5 The train-driver/The doctor at the hospital.

Appendix

Synopses of Readers used for exemplification

Animal Farm

Author	George Orwell
Publisher	Longman
Genre	Political satire
Series	The Bridge Series
Level	Upper Intermediate to Advanced
Headwords	3500
Activities	A2.4 A3.2 A4.1 B1.3 B4.1 C1.8 C2.1 C4.3

Summary
Mr Jones of Manor Farm is a lazy and thoughtless farmer, who is kicked off his farm by his animals. They rename the farm and begin to live by the principles of Animalism – 'All animals are equal'. As time goes by, the pigs obtain more privileges than the other animals, who find themselves in a worse position than when Jones was leader. In the final scene, the animals are unable to distinguish between the pigs and the humans who are visiting the farm.

Around the World in Eighty Days

Author	Jules Verne
Publisher	Oxford University Press
Genre	Picaresque adventure
Series	Oxford Progressive Readers
Level	Intermediate
Headwords	2900
Activities	B1.4 B4.3

Summary
Phileas Fogg, a punctilious English gentleman, accepts a wager that he cannot go around the world in eighty days. He immediately sets off with his new servant, Passepartout. His departure arouses the suspicions of Detective Fix, who believes Fogg to be a bank robber on the run. Fix sets off in pursuit of Fogg and almost causes him to lose his bet. Fogg finally arrives home despondent, believing that he has lost his wager. However, Passepartout discovers that Fogg has an extra day in hand because of the direction in which he travelled.

Don't Tell Me What To Do

Author	Michael Hardcastle
Publisher	Heinemann
Genre	Thriller
Series	Heinemann Guided Readers
Level	Elementary
Headwords	1100
Activities	A1.4

Summary

A young boy runs away from home to become a jockey. When he hitches a ride to London he is picked up by a wealthy man and his daughter. They want to take advantage of his small build and employ him to recover a bag of diamonds from a wrecked ship. The boy discovers that the small bag contains drugs, not diamonds and that others have previously died in the attempt to recover them. He is torn between his attraction to the daughter and his fear of the underwater task.

Hijacked

Author	J M Marks
Publisher	Oxford University Press
Genre	Thriller
Series	Alpha Books
Level	Intermediate
Headwords	1000
Activities	A1.1 A1.3 A2.2 A3.2 B4.3 C4.2 D

Summary

Jason Wright has been visiting his parents who live in the Far East. He is returning to his school in England when the plane is taken over by Japanese hijackers and the pilot is forced to land. The hijackers are holding various governments to ransom using the passengers as hostages. Jason, an accomplished swimmer, escapes from the plane and the remainder of the book deals with the methods used by Jason, the Japanese police and English Intelligence to foil the hijackers and release the hostages.

Outstanding Short Stories (*Lord Emsworth and the Girl Friend*)

Author	P G Wodehouse
Publisher	Longman
Genre	Humorous/human interest
Series	Longman Simplified English Series
Level	Upper Intermediate
Headwords	2000
Activities	C3.1

Summary
Lord Emsworth is Lord in name only. He is bullied by his gardener, Angus, and by his sister, Constance. Once a year, he holds a fête in the grounds of his stately home. Two of the visiting children, Gladys and Ern, are independent and spirited. Lord Emsworth shows kindness to Gladys and in return is invested with some of her spirit.

Outstanding Short Stories *(Lord Mountdrago)*
Author .   W Somerset Maugham
Genre   Mystery
Activities   D   E

Summary
Dr Audlin is a famous psychiatrist; Lord Mountdrago is a famous, but unpleasant politician. Lord Mountdrago visits Dr Audlin because he has been suffering from several unpleasant dreams. The dreams all involve Owen Griffiths, a rival politician, whom Mountdrago had needlessly humiliated in Parliament. The dreams are extremely vivid and degrading and, as a result, Mountdrago cannot relax or work. Griffiths appears as if he knows about the content of these dreams. Mountdrago does not keep his last appointment and the doctor reads in the paper that Owen Griffiths and Mountdrago died some distance apart, but within minutes of each other. The suggestion is that one caused the other's death, but *how* remains a mystery.

Outstanding Short Stories *(The Courtship of Susan Bell)*
Author   Anthony Trollop
Genre   Romance
Activities   A7.1   C2.1   C3.1

Summary
Mrs Bell, a widow, runs a genteel lodging house in Albany, New York State, in the nineteenth century. One of her guests, an engineer from New York City, falls in love with her younger daughter, Susan. The story tells of how the two are kept apart by the interference and narrow-mindedness of others, until finally, Aaron and Susan are reunited.

Outstanding Short Stories *(The Doll's House)*
Author   Katherine Mansfield
Genre   Human interest
Activities   A4.3   B3.2

Summary
The tale tells of the Burnell family, who have received a doll's house as a gift. They are the only children to own such a toy and it enables them to demonstrate their superiority over the other children. One of the poorest families in the community is the Kelvey family. The two Kelvey girls are ostracized by the rest of the community. Kezia Burnell allows the Kelvey girls to come and see the doll's house. Her act of generosity is discovered by her mother and she is punished.

Outstanding Short Stories (*The Man Who Could Work Miracles*)
Author   H G Wells
Genre   Mystery
Activities   B1.6   B1.7   B2.3   C1.1   C3.1

Summary
In some way, Fotheringay, a very ordinary man, obtains the power to
work miracles. He uses this power very badly and performs a lot of
silly, inconsequential acts until, finally, he stops the world revolving
and almost destroys the planet. Just in time, he wishes that his power
be removed and that all be as it was before. His power vanishes and all
is restored.

Outstanding Short Stories (*X-ing a Paragraph*)
Author   Edgar Allan Poe
Genre   Humorous
Activities   B3.3   C1.6   C3.3

Summary
A small town houses two rival newspapers. The two editors send
insulting messages to each other via the pages of their papers. The
feud heats up until, one day, the printer's boy finds that he has no Os
in stock. Traditionally, missing letters are substituted for by the letter
X. The boy substitutes X for every O in the paragraph. As the piece
has been written to include as many Os as possible the resulting article
is nonsense. The writer is so embarrassed that he leaves town.

Rich Man - Poor Man
Author   T C Jupp
Publisher   Heinemann
Genre   Human interest
Series   Heinemann Guided Readers
Level   Beginner
Headwords   600
Activities   A1.1   A2.6

Summary
A poor man, Adam, receives a money order from his son in England.
The story tells of Adam's struggles with bureaucracy in his attempts to
change the money order. Finally, he learns that the money order is
worthless and he is not so rich as he thought.

Rip Van Winkle
Author   Washington Irving
Publisher   Longman
Genre   Legend
Series   New Method Supplementary Readers
Level   Elementary
Headwords   750
Activities   B5.1

Summary
Rip Van Winkle falls asleep for twenty years. When he awakes he has no knowledge of the length of his sleep and he attempts to rejoin his community.

Scottish Adventure
Author   Richard Chisholm
Publisher   Heinemann
Genre   Thriller
Series   Heinemann Guided Readers
Level   Intermediate
Headwords   1600
Activities   B1.3   B1.4   B4.3

Summary
Mary refuses to sell her cottage to a wealthy landowner who wishes to open a climbing centre. As a result she is persecuted and terrified by the man's gang. When Mary's brother, John, comes to visit her the violence increases. John discovers that the climbing centre is a cover for a spy ring.

Silas Marner
Author   George Eliot
Publisher   Macmillan
Genre   Classic/human interest
Series   Stories to Remember
Level   Lower Intermediate to Advanced
Headwords   2000
Activities   A6.1   B1.1   B3.1   B4.2   D

Summary
Silas Marner, a weaver, comes to the remote village of Raveloe fifteen years before the story begins. He is bitter about his past and is made even more wretched when his savings are stolen. The lonely, old man receives custody of a baby girl, whose mother died outside his house one winter night. The child transforms his life and renews his hopes. Sixteen years later, the local squire claims the girl, Eppie, as his own daughter. Eppie refuses to leave Silas. His money is found and restored to him. Meanwhile, the squire must live with his guilt and shame.

Space Affair
Author   Peter Viney
Publisher   Oxford University Press
Genre   Science fiction
Series   Streamline Graded Readers
Level   Level four
Headwords   1250
Activities   A2.3

Summary
A space ship is on a journey which takes several years to complete. The crew of the ship works shifts. The Alpha shift never meet the Beta shift. However, Gareth falls in love with his Alpha counterpart, a woman he has never seen. They leave notes for each other at the end of their shifts and hope that they will not be caught. The penalty for communicating with other shift members is death.

Sunnyvista City

Author	Peter Viney
Publisher	Oxford University Press
Genre	Sci-fi romance
Series	Streamline Graded Readers
Level	Level three
Headwords	1000
Activities	B1.2

Summary
The story starts at a strange resort where nobody remembers very much about their past or why they have come on holiday. The guests are all drugged. One man, Dan, refuses to eat his food and slowly comes to his senses. He manages to escape and finds that the hotel is one of several similar places all over the world designed to solve a global unemployment problem.

Tales from the Arabian Nights *(The Unhappy King)*

Author	Retold by Rosemary Border
Publisher	Oxford University Press
Genre	Legend
Series	Oxford Progressive Readers
Level	Intermediate
Headwords	1400
Activities	A3.1

Summary
The king's wife was found with another man. The king ordered that she be executed immediately. After that, the king decided that his future wives would all be executed before they could stop loving him. So, on the day after every wedding they were executed. This continued on a daily basis until he married Scheherezade, who told the king a story which was never completed every night. The king was so anxious to hear these stories that he spared her life and grew to love her.

The Black Cat

Author	John Milne
Publisher	Heinemann
Genre	Crime thriller
Series	Heinemann Guided Readers
Level	Elementary
Headwords	1100
Activities	B1.4 B2.1

Summary
An ancient statue of a black cat is stolen from a tomb in Egypt. The cat may be gold. The police officer in charge pursues the gang from Egypt to Greece to Italy, until the cat is recovered.

The Piper of Hamelin

Author	Retold by Anthony Toyne
Publisher	Oxford University Press
Genre	Legend
Series	Oxford Graded Readers
Level	Elementary/Beginner
Headwords	750 (Junior)
Activities	A1.5 B2.1 C4.3

Summary
The town of Hamelin is infested with rats. One day, a stranger arrives who promises to rid the town of the rats if the Mayor will pay him a large sum. The Mayor agrees. The stranger plays unusual music on a pipe and the rats follow the music into the river and are drowned. The Mayor then refuses to pay the piper. To teach the Mayor a lesson the stranger plays his pipe again and, this time, all the children follow him to another land and are never seen again.

The Poseidon Adventure

Author	Paul Gallico
Publisher	Oxford University Press
Genre	Thriller
Series	Alpha Books
Level	Intermediate
Headwords	1000
Activities	A7.1 B1.4 C4.2 D

Summary
The cruise ship 'Poseidon' is caught in a tidal wave in the Aegean Sea. The ship capsizes and floats upside down. The only hope the survivors have is to climb upwards towards the keel before the ship fills with water and sinks. Two children, an elderly couple and a fanatic are included among the group who attempt to escape. The story tells of the dangers they encounter before the remaining members of their group are rescued.

The Stranger

Author	Norman Whitney
Publisher	Heinemann
Genre	Macabre
Series	Heinemann Guided Readers
Level	Elementary
Headwords	1100
Activities	A4.2 A5.1 B2.1

Summary
A small village is chosen as the location for a business venture of a very strange kind. Dave Slatin opens up a corner shop in the village of Woodend. The shop sells the usual produce, but Dave also has customers who come to ask him to solve their problems. Dave always gets what they want and obviously uses supernatural forces to do this.

The Thirty-Nine Steps

Author	John Buchan
Publisher	Longman
Genre	Thriller/mystery
Series	Longman Structural Readers
Level	Intermediate to Advanced
Headwords	2000
Activities	A2.1 A3.2 B1.2 C3.1 C3.2

Summary
The story takes place just before the First World War. A foreign government is planning to assassinate a leading politician in London. The only clue that Richard Hannay has is a notebook containing a message about thirty-nine steps given to him by a British agent just before his death. The foreign agents pursue Hannay to Scotland, believing that he knows more. The agents make it appeat that Hannay has committed the murders of which they are guilty, and therefore Hannay is also pursued by the police, who do not believe his story about the notebook. The final scene takes place at the Houses of Parliament where Hannay tries to prevent the minute hand of Big Ben reaching the point where a bomb will be detonated and Parliament destroyed.

According to the level selected the ending of the Reader may vary. The higher the level the more faithful is the Reader to Buchan's original ending which does not include the scene on Big Ben.

Recommended further reading

Boardman, R and **McRae, J**, *Reading Between the Lines* (Cambridge University Press, 1984).
Bouman, L, *Who's Afraid of Reading?*, Parts 1 & 2 in MET 12/3 and 12/4, 1985.
Carter, R and **Long, M**, *The Web of Words* (Cambridge University Press, 1987).
Gower, R and **Pearson, M**, *Reading Literature* (Longman, 1986).
Maley, A and **Moulding, S**, *Poem into Poem* (Cambridge University Press, 1986).